Medical Device Innovation Handbook

William K. Durfee and Paul A. Iaizzo, Editors
Medical Devices Center
University of Minnesota
Minneapolis, USA

UNIVERSITY OF MINNESOTA
Driven to Discover[SM]

MEDICAL DEVICE INNOVATION HANDBOOK

Medical Devices Center
University of Minnesota
Minneapolis, USA

This book is available as a free, full-color PDF download from
sites.google.com/a/umn.edu/mdih/
The print version can be purchased at cost at www.lulu.com.

Version: 4.0, November 9, 2016

Contents

Contributors

Ben Arcand Director, Medical Device Fellows Innovation Program, University of Minnesota, Minneapolis, USA

David Black Principal, Schwegman Lundberg & Woessner, P.A., Minneapolis, MN

William Durfee Professor, Department of Mechanical Engineering, University of Minnesota, Minneapolis, USA

Michael Finch Medical Industry Valuation Lab, Carlson School of Management, University of Minnesota, Minneapolis, USA

Mark Hjelle Product Line Manager, Heraeus Medical Components, Saint Paul, MN

Jenna Iaizzo ECT Program Manager, Medtronic, Minneapolis, Minnesota

Paul Iaizzo Professor, Department of Surgery, University of Minnesota, Minneapolis, USA

Barry Kudrowitz Assistant Professor, Product Design, College of Design, University of Minnesota, Minneapolis, USA

Tim Laske Vice President of Research and Business Development - Medtronic AF Solutions, Minneapolis, MN

1

Preface

This handbook was created to fill the need for a concise introduction to medical device innovation for those who are starting out, including students. Some of the material is based on innovation workshops held in Minneapolis and Tel Aviv, other material comes from the expertise of the contributing authors and still other material comes from the editors' experiences teaching undergraduate and graduate courses in medical device development. We thank all of the authors who have contributed material to this book.

The book was developed with the support of the University of Minnesota Medical Devices Center. For information about the center, see `www.mdc.umn.edu/`.

William K. Durfee
Paul A. Iaizzo

1 Innovation

William Durfee, University of Minnesota

innovation
Ideas that add value to society

1.1 Defining Innovation

The definition of innovation is about the introduction of something new, but is also about adding value.

Innovative products are new, useful and feasible. All three are needed for innovation. As you are thinking about your new idea, ask yourself, "Is my idea new?, "Is my idea useful, and if so, who will use it and for what purpose?," and "Is my idea feasible and if so, how will it be engineered and how will it be made?"

A theme that runs through this book is that the utility and value of the invention must be determined by the customer, not the inventor. This is a natural result of following a good innovation process, which starts with a problem to be solved where that problem is one that is experienced by the customer.

1.2 The Innovation Process

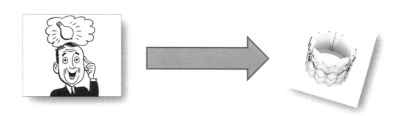

Later sections in this book cover the innovation process in detail, but here is a snapshot

1. Understand the opportunity
   Become knowledgeable about the disease state, the procedures currently used, the healthcare providers who participate and the problems and opportunities for improvement.

2. Define the need
   State, with some specificity, the customer need, where 'customer' could mean physician, nurse, patient, caregiver or other stakeholders.

3. Create solutions
   This is the inventive step where multiple concepts that solve the problem are created.

4. Assess the solutions
   The screening process where solutions are assessed to determine if they meet the need, if they are technically feasible and if they are economically viable. The result is down-selecting to one or two concepts to carry forward.

5. Further screens
   In addition to the screens in the step above, one must assess whether the concept can be patented, what the competition is doing, what it will take for the concept to be approved by regulatory agencies, what it will take for the concept to be reimbursed by third-party payers and what business model makes the most sense.

6. Build and test a prototype
   This is where the concept is realized as a physical prototype and bench tested to determine if it works. Later, pre-clinical animal testing on a more realistic prototype is used to refine the concept. If the device is intended to work external to the body, then animal testing is not needed and testing using human subjects can occur.

7. Carrying on
   Where the process goes from here is variable and depends on the concept and on the environment of the inventor. For example, the inventor could share their idea with an established medical devices company. Or, the inventor may be part of a medical device company already. Or, the inventor could decide to become or collaborate with an entrepreneur and start a new company based on the invention.

The key is to follow a needs-driven innovation process. In other words, first uncover the need, then invent to satisfy the need.

1.3 Medical Technology Innovation

The reason why medical technology innovation is needed is that new technology can add value by improving healthcare outcomes in some of the following ways.

- Better Procedures
  - Reduced procedure time
  - Improved procedure outcomes
  - Reduced procedure device costs
  - Fewer people in the procedure room
  - Efficient use of facilities
- Less Hospitalization
  - Faster recovery
  - Reduced re-hospitalizations
  - Moves patient care from clinic to home
- Improved Patient Satisfaction
  - Back to work and play faster
  - Home-based recovery
  - Improved health

A successful medical technology innovation depends on who is defining "success". The clinician-inventor wants to see their new device help patients. The med tech company wants to see market share. Investors want a return on their investment. Insurers want to lower the overall cost of healthcare. The innovator must recognize these sometimes conflicting drivers when considering their path.

1.4 Clinicians Becoming Innovators

"That doesn't mean we don't listen to customers, but it's hard for them to tell you what they want when they've never seen anything remotely like it. Take desktop video editing. I never got one request from someone who wanted to edit movies on his computer. Yet now that people see it, they say, 'Oh my God, that's great!'"
- Steve Jobs, Fortune, Jan. 2000

Innovative ideas often come from expert users who are most familiar with problems that need to be solved. This is particularly true for medical devices where clinicians and other health care providers conceive, by far, the largest number of ideas for new products to solve their problems. For example, a spinal cord injury doctor was acutely aware of the need for patients confined to their beds because of gluteal pressure ulcers, invented and followed through with the development of a prone cart with wheel-chair-like wheels so that patients could roll themselves around the hospital while maintaining their required prone position.

At the same time, creative health care professionals generally have little idea of what to do with their idea. They know their invention will solve a problem, but have no experience or training in what it takes to objectively evaluate their idea or how to move it through the commercialization process. The good news is that, as Chaim Lotan, Hadasah University Medical Center, says, "Innovation is a discipline that can be learned!"

One objective of this book is to help you bridge the gap from being simply an inventor to becoming an innovator, someone who can take an invention through the commercialization process. Knowledge of the innovation process plus capitalizing on the advice and assistance of experts is how the inventor becomes an innovator.

1.5 Trends

Med Tech Trends to Track

- Diagnostics that guide therapies
- From lab to desktop
- From clinic to home
- Physicians relieved of routine work
- Patients direct their healthcare
- Direct-to-patients apps
- Minimize hospital stay
- Better outcomes at lower cost!
- Evidence based outcomes
- No longer what solo doctor wants

It is a changing world for medical devices. In the past, if the doctor wanted it, the invention would become a successful product. Now, the device must satisfy a need, must lead to better outcomes and must be lower cost, all at the same time.

OLD	NEW
Clincal care rules	Economic value
Cost doesn't matter	Better outcomes at lower cost
Sell in the U.S.	Global market

The new environment is ripe for innovation. Connected health with portable devices and cloud-based data will drive care providing away from expensive clinical centers. Personalized healthcare will result from sensitive diagnostics and will lead to better outcomes. Big data will be mined for information to produce data-based effectiveness and cost metrics.

At the same time, the major disease drivers will not change. Chronic diseases and conditions such as diabetes, heart disease, cancer, obesity, stroke and arthritis affect about one half of all adults in the U.S. Heart disease and stroke cost $315 billion and arthritis and related conditions cost $128 billion [1]. Devices that address any of these conditions while meeting the new metrics present enormous opportunities for the innovator.

---

[1] CDC, *Chronic Diseases and Health Promotion*

2 Medical Device Product Development Process

William Durfee, University of Minnesota

2.1 Developing a Medical Device

Med Tech Development Process

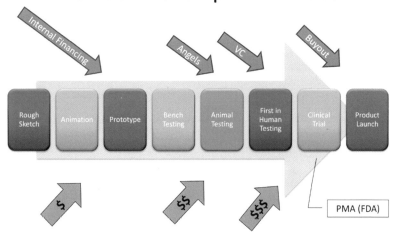

Generic Product Development Process

There are many new product development processes described in text books and company procedure documents. Most have steps that first involve a front-end of opportunity identification followed by concept development, and then move into steps of detailed product design and implementation followed by product launch and production ramp-up For example, many companies use the Stage-Gate process [1]. In some fast-paced industries (not medical), a

---

[1] www.stage-gate.com

company will rush a new product to launch without doing extensive prelim-inaries and then let the market decide success through sales. Consumer electronics such as cell phones and laptop computers fall into this category. For an overview of current thinking on product development process, see Katz [2].

Medical Device Product Development Process

Medical device product development has additional features that can domi-nate the process. Medical devices must pass a regulatory hurdle. To achieve a CE mark to market your product in Europe, you must prove that your de-vice is safe. To achieve FDA approval to market your device in the U.S., you must prove that your device is safe and effective. If your device is completely new and comes with a level of risk to the patient, lengthy and costly clinical trials will likely be needed to obtain regulatory approval. Even if your de-vice passes the regulatory hurdle, you must prove to reimbursement agents (medical insurers and government medical agencies) that your device low-ers the procedure cost and improves patient outcomes sufficiently to warrant reimbursement. Without reimbursement, your device will not be successful because few patients can afford a large out-of-pocket expense for a medical procedure.

The diagram at the beginning of this chapter illustrated the main stages of how a typical medical device is developed. The opportunity identification and the initial concept often comes from a clinician who is intimately familiar with a clinical problem that needs solving, and might have a rough concept sketch on a napkin. As the design is refined, renderings and animations are developed to communicate the concept to customers and investors. Low-resolution physical prototypes are created to work out some of the details, followed by initial bench testing to study engineering performance. All of these steps are low cost and typically financed internally.

Next comes testing in animals, first-in-human testing and clinical trials, fol-lowed by regulatory approval, reimbursement decisions and product launch. Each step is progressively more expensive and financing becomes a ma-jor consideration. For example, for a start-up with an FDA Class III (life-supporting) device, it costs about $150M to take the company through the FDA PMA process [3].

---

[2]G. Katz, Rethinking the Product Development Funnel, available at http://goo.gl/pZ1HV
[3]VC Roundtable, The Collaborative, Star Tribune, http://goo.gl/YS5xu

Medical Device Innovation Process

Med-Tech <u>Innovation</u> Process

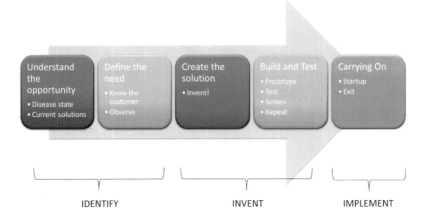

Another view of the process is shown in med-tech innovation figure, which has innovation split into five broad tasks, which can be further reduced to Identify, Invent, Implement stages as popularized by the process described in the Biodesign text [4]

The Importance of Teams

Habits of Effective Product Development Teams

- Studies the customer
- Creative
- Not afraid to prototype
- Can evaluate objectively
- Is cross-functional
- Has an established development process
- Manages risk, abandons project if necesary

[4]Zenios, Makower, Yock, Brinton, Kumar, Watkins, Denend, Krummel (2015). *Biodesign: the process of innovating medical technologies*, 2nd ed. Cambridge University Press.

Leading innovative companies such as Black & Decker and IDEO all have an effective product development process. While the processes may vary in their details, their teams share the characteristics listed above. On the list, "study the customer" is at the top because a deep understanding of the market opportunity gained through a comprehensive, critical, first-hand study of the customer is the most important factor for developing a successful product.

Effective teams are even more important for medical device development where expertise is needed across a broad spectrum. For starters, your core team should involve one who has a deep understanding of the clinical problem, one with relevant engineering expertise and one with knowledge and experience in entrepreneurship and startup businesses. As your development process proceeds, you will likely need to add others to the team including experts in clinical trials, regulatory and reimbursement, among other specialties.

2.2 Feasibility Screening

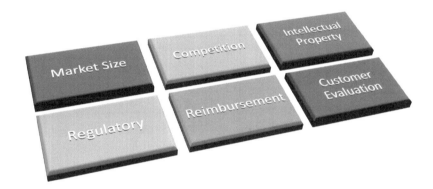

When developing your idea, even at the early stages, continually test it for feasibility, which are the screening criteria used within a med tech company to screen ideas for internal product development and also used by investors to determine what to fund. Broadly, screening criteria fall into three categories:

Market Feasibility Does anyone want it?
Technical Feasibility Can we make it?
Financial Feasibility Can $ be made?

To determine market feasibility, discover the specific problem to be solved, define who will use your solution, find out if those who will use your solution actually like your idea and then make an estimate of how large the market is. To determine technical feasibility, build and test a prototype. To determine financial feasibility, estimate the fully burdened cost of the project, estimate an appropriate selling price and project sales growth. In addition, estimate the time and money it will take to get from where your are now to product launch. Creating realistic financial pro formas for a med tech product is challenging. If you are not a med tech finance person, consult with an expert on this step.

Finally, even if the product meets the the three broad criteria, the project must fit the organization you are pitching to. For example, a company whose core competency is hip implants is not going be interested in a neuromodulation device.

Evaluation of Medical Device Concepts

For medical device concepts, the specific evaluation screens are shown in the figure that opened this section:

Market Size What is the size of the disease state and how much of that market can be captured?

Competition How are people solving the problem now and what do med tech competitors (established companies and startups) have now and what are they going to have five years from now?

Intellectural Property Have patents been filed and is there freedom to operate?

Regulatory What will it take to get regulatory approval?

Reimbursement What is the reimbursement path?

Customer Evaluation Do the users like the concept?

In addition, the technology must have a clear development path that can take the concept to a finished product, including manufacturing scale-up without excessive basic research. Finally, investors will use all of these criteria to assess the potential scale of and timing for return on investment for the opportunity.

2.3 Why the Process Might Fail

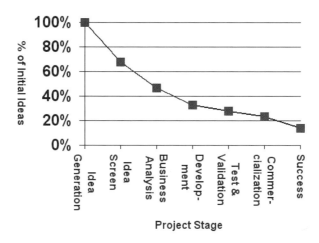

About 40% of new products fail post-launch

Source: www.pdma.org

Products, including new medical devices fail to take off when innovators:

1. Were focused on features not benefits
2. Did not understand the market need
3. Projected an optimistic time to product launch or a ramp up of sales that was too steep
4. Had an idea that was before its time

3 Understanding the Opportunity

Ben Arcand, Medical Devices Center

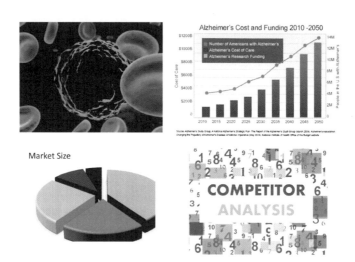

Alzheimer's Cost and Funding 2010 -2050

Market Size

COMPETITOR ANALYSIS

Once a compelling clinical need has been identified, it can be tempting to jump directly to developing solution concepts. However, it is imperative that in-depth understanding of important information about the opportunity is achieved. This includes understanding the disease and how it is currently treated, what the market size for the opportunity and what competitors are doing. This understanding will be critical for high-level VOC discussions with physicians and for future refinement of concepts.

3.1 Researching the Disease State

Researching the disease state can be broken down into 4 areas:

Anatomy Structure and naming of the relevant organs and tissues. Also the variety and variances of these structures in the population.

Physiology & Pathophysiology Physiology deals with the function of organs and tissues and pathophysiology with the disfunction of organs and tissues due to disease.

14

Epidemiology Prevalence, incidence and distribution of a disease. Prevalence is the proportion of a population found to have a condition while the incidence is the rate of occurrence of a disease in a population over a time period (usually 1 yr). The distribution of the disease among different segments of a population such as men vs women or different age ranges is also important.

Care Pathway Diagnosis, referral to specialists, treatments performed and outcomes of treatments.

Anatomy

Gaining a deep understanding of the anatomical structures and nomenclature will be invaluable when discussing need and solutions with clinicians. Additionally, information on sizes and variations will be needed for designing potential solutions.

Physiology & Pathophysiology

Function, and dysfunction in the case of disease, is essential knowledge if you are to develop solutions to move towards a cure or reduction of symptoms. How a disease presents in the clinic, with what symptoms, and how the final diagnosis is made all inform on how a patient will move through the care system and ultimately to a treatment. Understanding the comorbities that typically present with the disease, for example obesity or other diseases, will inform on some of the challenges that may need to be met when designing a solution.

Epidemiology

The rates of incidence and prevalence reported in literature can be highly variable depending on methods used and the population that was studied. Careful reading may be required to understand why one researcher reports several times the prevalence rate of another researcher. A meta-analysis that retrospectively assesses past research can be useful in understanding these results, if available. In any case, a range of the number of patients currently suffering from a disease (prevalence) and the rate at which new patients are acquiring a disease (incidence) will be necessary to assess the importance and potential market for a solution.

Care Pathway

The care pathway is a concept describing how a disease is identified in a patient, by what care professionals, in what clinical setting, how that disease is treated and the outcomes of those treatments. This information can be critical for crafting how and where a solution may be administered and by what type of practitioner. Often a disruptive new solution to a clinical need may involve changing how a disease is identified, or the setting and by whom administers a treatment. Equally important is an understanding how patients drop out of the care pathway through frustration, cost or a lack of results. Below is an example care pathway assessment for treatment of individuals with chronic sinusitis.

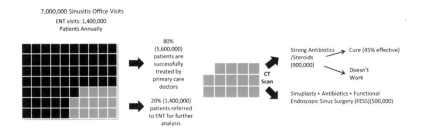

Resources

PubMed A free resource that is developed and maintained by the National Center for Biotechnology Information (NCBI), at the U.S. National Library of Medicine (NLM), located at the National Institutes of Health (NIH). It is the most comprehensive database of peer-reviewed academic literature. Easy to use.

MedlinePlus Tutorials on health conditions and diseases. A service of the NIH National Library of Medicine.

NIH Each institute of NIH has a resource page that describes the basics of disease and disorders relevant to that institute. For example NINDS on its "Disorders A-Z" page has tutorials on every known neurological disorder.

Videos of Surgical Procedures Along with internet searches, Medline Plus maintains a comprehensive set of links to high-quality videos of surgical procedures.

UpToDate A subscription resource that is continuously updated by over 5,100 physicians to ensure the content stays current.

3.2 Sizing the Market

Most medical device innovators get into this field because of an underlying desire to help patients and have a positive impact on healthcare and
medicine. Profit is not usually the prime motivator. However, developing
a medical device is typically a long-term and expensive proposition that requires a comparable potential for market size and sales to justify making the
large up-front investment.

Understanding the market and potential return on investment is therefore
an essential part of evaluating whether to work towards a potential solution to
an unmet clinical need. If the potential innovation wont survive as a successful product, then it wont exist or be available long enough to help patients and
doctors.

Much of the epidemiological and clinical pathway data uncovered when researching the disease state is used to analyze and estimate market sizes. In
the following figure, the care pathway and epidemiological data for overactive
bladder is outlined in an inverted pyramid diagram showing the segmentation
towards the likely patient/market segment. In this case, out of the estimated
19.7 million people with overactive bladder in the U.S., 7.2 million are di-
agnosed and only 20k and 247k being treated surgically or successfully by
pharmaceuticals respectively.

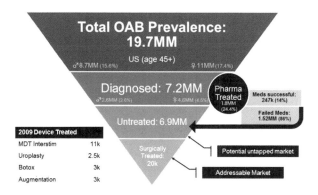

For this example, the purpose of this unmet clinical need is for a better surgical solution. This leaves 6.9 million patients untreated which would equate
to an untapped potential market and 20k as the current addressable market
for those currently selecting surgical solutions to their OAB. If we estimate a
potential price for the solution (based on costs of current solutions), we can
get rough market estimates that can be later refined as more is learned. In
this case, the market currently supports about $1,000 for surgical devices
making.

Current market size: 20k * $1000 = $20M market

Potential market size: 6.9M * $1000 = $6.9 B

As rule of thumb, a market size that will support the cost of development and clinical trials for a PMA device is at least $500M. Refinement of the market size estimates can be achieved as a better idea on the patient segment, cost-of-goods (COGS) for the solution and the business model are developed.

Resources

3.3 Analyzing the Competition

An examination of the competitive solutions that are currently available and under development will help in the refinement of your business model and clearly differentiate how features of your innovation will provide for a better solution and compete for market share when available. Through literature searches and voice-of-the-customer interviews, a number of products, pharmaceuticals, treatments and surgical techniques have most likely surfaced. The various attributes of each solution should be cataloged in a simple table that might include these headings: Cost, Features and Attributes, Caregiver, Special Training Required, Pros/Cons, Outcomes, Where Treatment Performed, Patient Segment Treated, Business Model (e.g. single use, capital equipment, marketing strategy), Market Share (rough estimate).

Here is a generic example for exploring opportunities in the overactive bladder space.

Product	Features	Venue	Outcomes
Implantable stimulator	Minimally invasive surgery. Screening step. Low effectiveness.	O.R.	60% efficacy
Percutaneous tibial nerve	No surgery or drug side effects. Multiple visits needed.	Office	77% moderate improvement
Botox injections	Reversible and minimally invasive. Off label use. Continuous injections needed. Low effectiveness.	Office	12-50% efficacy
Implantable drug delivery	Single visit for long dosing. Effectiveness TBD.	Office?	TBD
Bladder balloon	Office implantable device. Removable. Effectiveness TBD.	Office?	TBD
Bladder replacement	New organ created from patient cells. Major surgery.	O.R.	TBD

Resources

ClinicalTrials.gov A comprehensive, searchable database of federally and privately supported clinical trials in the U.S. and around the world. A good way of finding out what the competition is doing.

4 Human Anatomy and Physiology

Paul Iaizzo, University of Minnesota

It is critical for medical devices designers to:

- Learn terminology and anatomic, physiologic and pathophysiologic principles.

- Analyze images and procedures from clinical cases.

- Study anatomical specimens.

- Consult with clinical and anatomical experts.

- Develop 3D models of relevant anatomy and devices.

- Use computer simulations.

Learning Anatomical, Physiological and Pathophysiological Terminology

There are many anatomical terms that the medical device designer should be familiar with as they start the process of device innovation. For example, the designer must be able to identify the standard human anatomic position and anatomic planes to describe body locations (Fig. 4.1.) Regardless of the position of the body or organ upon examination, the anatomy of an organ or the whole should be described as if observed from the vantage point of the standard anatomic position. The standard position is divided by three orthogonal planes: (1) the sagittal plane, which divides the body into right and left portions; (2) the coronal plane, which divides the body into anterior and posterior portions; and (3) the transverse plane, which divides the body into superior and inferior portions. Another example of top-level anatomy is the relative location of the human heart within the ribcage as shown in Fig. 4.2.

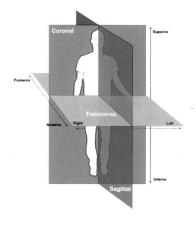

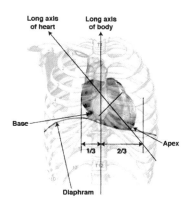

Figure 4.1: Anatomic planes. (From Hill, 2015.)

Figure 4.2: Relative location of the heart in the thorax.

Learning Anatomy

There are numerous avenues for studying human anatomy and gaining expertise relevant to your technology. University courses, websites and textbooks (some dating back hundreds of years that can be fun to explore) are just some of those avenues. The classic Netter textbooks with their excellent anatomical drawings are an excellent place to start. One example of a university-based resource is the advanced cardiac anatomy and physiology week-long short course held every January at the University of Minnesota. If you are working at a large company you should seek out in-house expertise. Human anatomy is highly variable and can be further modified by disease and by various treatments. Thus, one must study the full range of anatomy that might be seen by the proposed device both pre and post treatment.

For example, if you need to understand the relative association of the cardiovascular system relative to lymphatic system, there are many such good depictions such as the one shown in Fig. 4.3. Or, if developing a device that works on the brain, the "Handbook of Neural Engineering" is a good starting point for learning detailed anatomy. Examples from this book include Fig. 4.4, which shows general brain structure, and Fig. 4.5, which shows the anatomical and physiological differences within the autonomic nervous system.

Ideally, one should study an array of human anatomical specimens associated with the proposed therapy, including both pre and post-therapy specimens. Yet, this can be difficult to accomplish and can entail major expense. Instead, a good place to start is to dissect and study appropriate animal models. For example, one can learn much about human cardiac anatomy by dissecting swine hearts, which can be obtained from a local butcher shop at low cost.

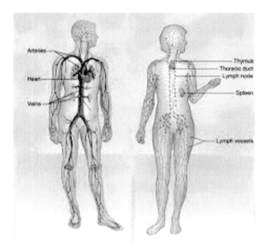

Figure 4.3: The major components of the cardiovascular system: blood, blood vessels, heart, and lymphatic system. (Left) Major vessels that return blood to the heart (blue) and major arteries that leave the heart (red). (Right) The lymphatic system. (from Iaizzo, 2015).

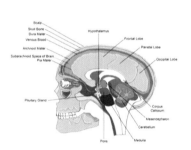

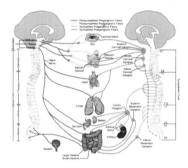

Figure 4.4: Major areas within the brain. (From Iaizzo, 2013.)

Figure 4.5: Sympathetic and parasympathetic divisions of the autonomic nervous system. Divisions may innervate the same organ but have different effector responses. (from Iaizzo, 2013).

Computational and Physical Models

Computational modeling is a useful tool for clinicians and device designers to better understand associated anatomies that may lead to optimization of therapeutic treatments. In addition, physical models derived from medical imaging can be a valuable design tool. For example, the Visible Heart® laboratory at the University of Minnesota has developed 3D printed models for education that have been presented at scientific meetings around the world and have been given to physicians to aid in patient education. The group also uses 3D printing to create scaled-up models of specific structures to better understand complex anatomies, which can be particularly important in pediatric cases (Fig. 4.6). Prototype cardiac devices can be placed and tested in a soft printed silicon heart with varying anatomy and pathologies as an analog to human specimens.

Another example of how 3D printed models can be used to learn anatomy is shown in Fig. 4.7 where lab students are hand-painting anatomical models. This is the 3D analog of the popular "Anatomy Coloring Book" and is a way to understand detailed cardiac structures and how varied they can be.

Figure 4.6: Human Heart 083 model from a 56 year old male with no known cardiac history, yet the model shows a slight degree of left ventricular hypertrophy. Heart was perfusion-fixed then MRI scanned (left). From the MRI image, the heart was 3D printed with coronary arteries highlighted in black (right). (from Iaizzo, 2016)

Figure 4.7: Students learning anatomy by hand painting 3D printed models of human hearts. (from Iaizzo, 2016)

Summary

For you are planning to develop a medical device or therapy, it is critical that you learn all appropriate associated terminology as well as the underlying anatomic, physiologic and pathophysiologic principles. You should as quickly become an engaged student of these topics, utilizing all available internal and external resources possible. Try to gain access to associated anatomical specimens, which may be accomplished via specified University courses, and try to gain access to images from clinical cases. Also, try yourself to dissect the appropriate animal tissues for the associated anatomies, for example by obtaining specimens from a butcher shop. Throughout your educational journey, consult with clinical and anatomical experts. With recent advances in 3D anatomical modeling and computer simulations, much value can be gained by virtual prototyping of the implantation of your medical device or application of your therapy in a variety of human anatomies. Throughout your medical device career, to remain successful, you should be a vigilant student of human anatomy and physiology.

Further Reading

The website for this handbook (see Page ii) has a list of resources for learning about anatomy and physiology.

5 Discovering Needs

William Durfee, University of Minnesota

Understanding Customer Needs

"If I had asked my customers what they wanted, they would have told me a faster horse."

Henry Ford

This often told quote may not have been actually spoken by Ford (history is uncertain), but certainly represents Ford's philosophy about product development. Here is similar quote from Steve Jobs that is true: "That doesn't mean we don't listen to customers, but it's hard for them to tell you what they want when they've never seen anything remotely like it. Take desktop video editing. I never got one request from someone who wanted to edit movies on his computer. Yet now that people see it, they say, 'Oh my God, thats great!' " (Fortune, 24 Jan. 2000).

Customer input, sometimes called voice of the customer (VOC), at a minimum should come at three stages when developing your idea. Initially market research is conducted to understand customer needs and to identify the problem to be solved. This typically involves one-on-one interviews and observations of the target user in their environment.

Next market research is conducted to get customer reaction to your concept. This important stage comes after you have chosen, but not refined your idea. Input from the customer can help you to determine if you are on the right track and how to improve your idea.

Finally, market research is conducted to get reaction to your working prototype. In this stage you are gathering data on what target customers like and dont like about your product. The data will be more valuable if the prototype can be used by customers.

5.1 Defining the Customer

Who Is the Customer?

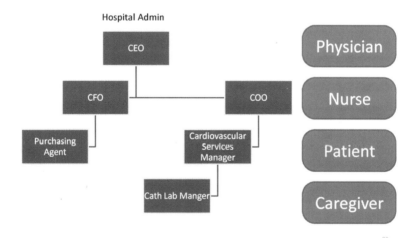

With medical technology, one of the first steps is to determine who is the customer because only then can you begin the task of understanding the needs of the customer.

5.2 Market Research

Market Research Methods

Qualitative

- To measure what customers are thinking and why
- One-on-one interviews and observations
- Data reported using summary statements and customer quotes
- Used in early stages of project

Quantitative

- To measure how many
- Large sample surveys: online, mail, telephone
- Data reported using summary statistics
- Used in later stages of project
- Less control over respondent demographics

Recommendation 1: Interviews Conduct 10 to 20 qualitative, in-depth interviews. In person or by telephone. Appropriate because, unlike quantitative research it is exploratory and flexible. Individual interview because, unlike focus groups, they are easier to execute, particularly if you are low on cash.

Recommendation 2: User observations Observe user in their work environment to understand current concerns. Ask occasional why are you doing it this way? questions, but mostly use your eyes to gather information. For example, if you are designing a new IV pole, tag along behind a nurse, including to the storage closet where the poles are stored.

Recommendation 3: Quantitative Survey If quantitative market data is required, hire a market research company to conduct for you. Resist the urge to put a quick survey up on the Internet. Good quantitative research requires expertise in designing the right questions and considerable effort to get right demographics in the response set.

5.3 Using Interviews

Defining the Need

Look for pain points

Interview Customers
"Why is that a problem for you?"

Personal Experience
"Why is that a problem for me?"

A major issue or an
inconvenience?

How many have the
same need?

How is it done now?

One-on-one interviews are the most useful (and least costly) way to gather input on customer needs. The advantage of an interview is that you can probe with follow-ups and can steer the interview depending on who you are talking with and what they are saying.

Interview Methods

- Determine the research <u>objective</u>
  - What do you want to get out of the interview?
- Determine interview targets
  - Job description, level of experience
  - Who you want to talk to and who you don't want to talk to
  - Key opinion leaders may only represent 5% of the market
- Find interviewees
- Prepare the interview guide
- Conduct the interviews
- Analyze and report results

The most important aspect of gathering user input through interviews is to determine the purpose of the interviews. For example, what business decisions will be driven by the research results? Which questions are mission critical and which are just nice to know?

Developing for key opinion leaders may result in a complex product that can only be used in academic centers, limiting market share.

The interview guide outlines topic areas for the questions. It is used by the interviewer to guide the conversation. The interviewer deviates from the guide depending on where the conversation goes. Prepare the guide in light of knowing how much time you expect to have with the interviewee.

When conducting the interview, start and end on time. Avoid bias: "I like this solution, what do you think?," and avoid questions outside of the interviewee expertise: "What would you pay for this?" Probe with follow-up questions to get depth and to get the why that underlies their opinion: "What do you mean by ...." "Tell me more about ...." "What makes you say that ... will not work?"

If testing a concept, report, without selling, who the concept is for and what the concept does. Avoid bias in your description. Get their overall reaction, their likes and their dislikes.

5.4 Creating Needs Statements

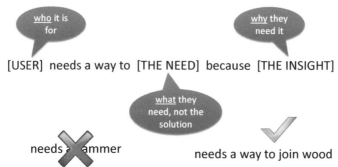

Robert, an interventional cardiologist, needs a way to stay alert all day because he finds himself booked with too many patients.

After you have gathered customer input through interviews and on-site observations, a useful way to form conclusions about what you found out is by creating a list of needs. From there, screen and combine to end up with one or two needs that (1) are related to a specific and significant problem, (2) are feasible to be met through an inventive process (3) if met will lead to a significant improvement in a health care procedure or outcome and (4) are connected to a significant market opportunity.

From your narrowed list of needs, convert into one or two structured needs statements as suggested by the template in the figure. Well-crafted needs statements can be used in all the following phases of the innovation process and are particularly useful when screening ideas. Remember that the final needs statements must be backed up by the evidence gathered from your customer and disease state research.

6 Generating and Screening Ideas

Barry Kudrowitz, University of Minnesota

6.1 Generating Ideas

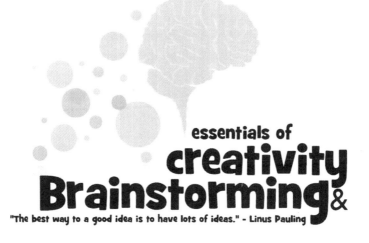

essentials of
creativity
Brainstorming&
"The best way to a good idea is to have lots of ideas." - Linus Pauling

There are many methods for generating ideas. You can borrow ideas of others by studying patents and tearing down competing products. You can solo-storm by yourself in a quiet place with just you and your sketchbook, to unleash your own ideas. Or, you can brainstorm with a group to get many ideas quickly. In all cases, you goal is to generate many ideas because the more ideas you have, the more good ideas you will have [1].

---

[1]Kudrowitz and Wallace (2013). Assessing the quality of ideas from prolific, early-stage product ideation. Journal of Engineering Design, 24(2), 120-139.

6.2 Brainstorming

Brainstorm

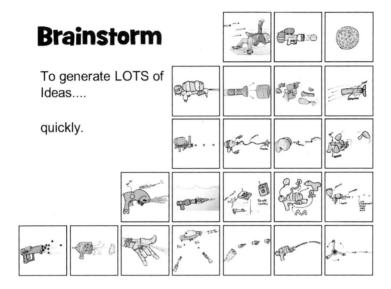

To generate LOTS of Ideas....

quickly.

The goal of brainstorming is to generate lots of ideas ... quickly. Brainstorming works best with a group of 5-9 people working for 20-40 minutes.The session length needs to be long enough to go past the initial burst of ideas, but no so long that participants are exhausted. Note that many of the best ideas come out at the end of the session when exhaustion is about to set in. A round table is ideal. Appoint a facilitator and have lots of paper. A facilitator is needed to provide periodic bursts of energy and encouragement to participants. It helps to not invite the boss because bosses by nature are critical and opinionated, two traits that need to be suppressed during brainstorming.

Brainstorming Rules

In short; there are no rules. And here they are [2]

Rule 1: Defer Judgment Deferring judgment is the most difficult aspect for those new to brainstorming because it is so easy to shoot down an idea. "Oh that will never work," is the fastest way to kill off a brainstorming session as the owner of the idea will immediately become self conscious. Another reason to defer judgment is that if you stop to evaluate each idea, you will never have time to generate a lot of ideas. So,

---

[2]McCloud, S. (2006). Making Comics: Storytelling Secrets Of Comics, Manga And Graphic Novels.

when a member of your brainstorming group presents an idea that you think is awesome or dumb, your job is to smile, say "great idea" and move on.

A corollary to defer judgment is "silly ideas are good." That is because the silly idea is often the one that triggers the money-winning idea.

Defer judgment is also at the heart of the "How Might We" concept, which is described in a 2012 Harvard Business Review article [3]. Here the idea is that saying "How might we improve X," leads to participation by all ('we') and to the concept of deferring judgment ('might'.) How might we prompts can be used to trigger brainstorming sessions, for example, "How might we improve the patient experience in the phlebotomy lab?"

Rule 2: Build on Ideas Building on an idea you just heard is an exceptionally powerful means to trigger new ideas. "Yes, and ..." must be encouraged as a positive way to build on the ideas of others. "Yes, I like your idea and we could also do this ..."

Brainstorming Tips

Brainstorm Sketching

One idea/page

Quick and clear

Draw Big and bold

Title the idea

Brief pitch

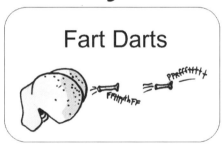

Have markers and paper or large Post-It notes. Every idea gets a quick sketch and a title, but don't take the time to explain every idea in detail.

[3]http://goo.gl/hM6sH

There are many short improv activities that are excellent ways to warm up for a brainstorming session and have been proven to lead to sessions that generate up to 36% more ideas. This is just like stretching before an athletic event. Improv warmups can enable bonding, lower inhibitions, encourage wild ideas and improve listening skills.

After the session it is revealing to compute the ideas per minute per person (IPMPP) resulting from the session. Creative types do over 1.0 IPMPP in a session. (1.0 IPMPP is 5 people generating 100 ideas in 20 minutes.)

For more on brainstorming view this video resource: `http://goo.gl/QGTdHk`

6.3 Sorting Ideas

A good brainstorming session will generate dozens, or even better hundreds, of ideas. Before screening, it can be helpful to sort the ideas into themes. One method for initial sorting is Affinity Diagrams [4] (also known as the KJ Method).

In the Affinity Diagram method, the idea cards are spread out on the table or wall. Participants are told to take two ideas that appear to be related and place them together in an empty part of the table. Then anyone can move addition items into that group. If someone's group does not seem to make sense, anyone can re-arrange the group or can move ideas from one group to another, or to a new group. The whole process is done without talking or discussion. The result is that categories grow organically and by implied consensus. The process continues until most of the idea cards are in a group and participants have stopped moving cards from group to group.

The next step is for each participant to create a name or short phrase to each group. The names are disclosed all at the same time to prevent being biased by other participants and to force every participant to review the ideas in every group. Once all the proposed names are exposed, the group can then discuss and come to consensus on a single name. Sometimes that process will result in two groups being combined.

When complete, the team will have their ideas sorted into named categories. This makes the process of screening ideas more efficient. Keep in mind that this step is only for managing a large number of ideas, not for screening, selecting or killing ideas.

---

[4] `http://en.wikipedia.org/wiki/Affinity_diagram`

6.4 Screening Ideas

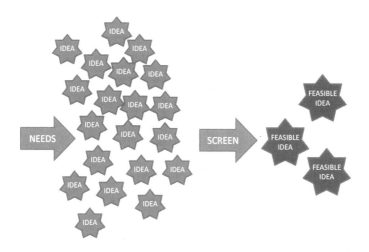

A good ideation process will result in dozens or hundreds of ideas that meet the need. Now comes the time to do an initial screen. This is a three step process. First, agree on a list of criteria by which ideas will be judged. Second, apply the criteria to each idea. Third, from the rating results, determine which two to four ideas are worthy of further investigation. It is generally better at this stage to screen to a small set of ideas rather than narrowing down to one idea. During the screening process, it is common to extract features from rejected ideas and add them to the ideas that pass the screen.

The basic metrics used for screening relate to the feasibility filters described in Section 2.2. While dozens of screening criteria could be applied, try to prune your initial list of criteria down to the six or so that are the most significant for product success.

For medical technology, criteria related to objective health care outcomes must be included. For example, reduced procedure time, better use of clinical facilities, reduced hospitalization time, increased patient safety, increased patient comfort or confidence, reduced cost. Additional criteria must include whether the concept can be patented, pass through regulatory hurdles, be reimbursed and have a feasible business model for commercialization.

Multi-Voting

While not recommended for a rigorous selection, one method for conducting an initial or even final screen is multi-voting. Here, all ideas are placed on the table or stuck to the wall. Each participant is given five green and five red sticky dots. Without discussion, participants review the ideas and place their green dots on ideas they like and red dots on ideas they think should be killed. A participant can put more than one dot on an idea. For example, if they *really* like one idea, all five of their green dots could go on that idea. Participants also don't have to use all their dots.

When done, the team can step back and get a view of whether there is any consensus on the ideas. The danger is that this method is based on intuition and therefore should not be the only means of making selections.

For more on concept screening view this video resource: `http://goo.gl/PGqiBU`

7 Testing Your Idea

Paul Iaizzo

7.1 Bench Testing

Start by Bench Testing Your Device

- Optimize product design
- Simulate various clinical anatomies
- Accelerated wear testing
- Ongoing verification as to the utility of a technology
- Freeze design before pre-clinical studies are initiated

Bench testing is low cost and is used to validate the engineering function of your device before committing to more costly animal and human studies. Often, early bench testing for small products is done on a bench version that is scaled up in size.

In developing a test plan for the bench tests, determine the key objectives of the study, anticipate the desired results and plan the protocols accordingly.

Bench testing in tissue analogs is also useful. For example, some medical products are first bench tested in chicken breast or beef liver obtained from the local supermarket.

7.2 Animal Testing

Animal Model Tests

- To validate efficacy of a device within an appropriate animal model.
- To validate device in real anatomy and physiology
- To obtain outcomes and safety data needed for 510(k) submissions or for developing human clinical trials
- To obtain bio-compatibility data
- To gain confidence in the technology itself

The goal of pre-clinical animal studies is to decrease the number of iterations before moving to clinical studies in humans. While bench testing can indicate whether the engineering performance of a device meets target specifications, only animal testing can reveal whether the device has the anticipated biological or physiological effects. The main limitation of animal testing is that it cannot provide a definitive statement regarding safety and efficacy of your device in humans. Because animal testing is expensive and time consuming, do everything you can to use bench tests for initial device validation.

In planning for animal testing, first identify the risk areas for the product. This might be materials, principle of operation, endurance or placement procedure, and then design a test plan to validate each risk. Because animal model testing results will likely be submitted to the regulatory agency as evidence for safety and efficacy, be thinking of regulatory guidelines from the start, including the requirements for good laboratory practices (GLP) as defined by U.S. federal law. Animal testing for many devices have regulatory requirements and standards. For example stent testing generally uses a classic porcine coronary injury model, and cardiac valve testing is covered by ISO 5840. Advanced animal model studies should happen after the device has passed a design freeze stage.

Picking the Animal Model

Pick the appropriate animal model. Study can be in intact animal or in isolated organ. For example, if you are developing a new heart device, here are the choices you have for testing:

1. Human hearts in vivo
2. Human hearts in vitro
3. Large mammalian hearts in vivo
4. Large mammalian hearts in vitro
5. Isolated perfused hearts
6. Isolated muscle preparations
7. Isolated cells
8. Subcellular fractions

Lower numbers on the list result in data that is highly relevant but comes at high cost and fewer samples. Higher numbers on the list are the opposite. If the purpose of the animal testing is proof of concept than innovative animal models can be used. If the purpose is to provide data to the FDA and is part of GLP testing then a standard model should be used.

8 Clinical Trials

Jenna Iaizzo, Medtronic

Clinical Research and Testing

- To test elements of clinical practice
- To justify clinical decisions
- To optimize the device
- To provide safety and efficacy data for FDA submission

8.1 Introduction

Clinical trials are a necessary step in the medical device innovation process and are the only way that the developer can determine how the device will perform in the human body or when used by humans. A clinical trial provides valid scientific evidence on the safety and efficacy of a device, which can be used when submitting to a regulatory body for approval to market or to a third party payer when making the case for reimbursement.

Early clinical testing, sometimes called first-in-human (FIH) tests, are studies with a small number of subjects (one to 10) to do initial validation of the device in humans. Larger validation studies can involve hundreds of subjects and multiple trial sites around the country or around the world. Any clinical study requires clearly defined objectives, a repeatable protocol, appropriate statistics to analyze results and honest interpretation of the data. Startups and established med-tech companies often contract with universities to conduct early stage clinical research and to assist with full-blown clinical trials.

All research using human subjects requires examination and approval by a local Institutional Review Board (IRB) in the U.S., whose counterpart in other countries is the Ethics Committee. The role of the IRB is to determine that the protocol is appropriate, the benefits of the study outweigh the risks, investigators are qualified and trained in the principles of research involving human subjects, subject participation in voluntary and principles of informed consent will be followed. Most research universities have a local IRB with extensive guidance to investigators on local requirements and protocol submission and approval process.

8.2 Good Clinical Practice

Principles of Good Clinical Practice

Ethics
1. Ethical conduct of clinical trials
2. Benefits justify risks
3. Rights, safety, and well-being of subject prevail

Protocol & Science
4. Nonclinical and clinical information supports the trial
5. Compliance with a scientifically sound, detailed protocol

Responsibilities
6. IRB approval prior to initiation
7. Medical care and decisions made by qualified physician
8. Each person qualified through education and training to perform their tasks

Informed Consent
9. Freely given by every subject prior to participation

Data Quality & Integrity
10. Accurate reporting, interpretation, and verification
11. Protects confidentiality of records

Investigational Products
12. Conform to Good Manufacturing Practice and used per protocol

Quality Control & Assurance
13. Systems with procedures to ensure quality of every aspect of the trial

Source: FDA

The FDA defines what is known has Good Clinical Practice (GCP), a set of principles that should and must be followed for any clinical study that will be used as evidence for regulatory approval. GCP is the standard for the design, conduct, performance, monitoring, auditing, recording, analysis and reporting of clinical studies. GCP is intended to protect the rights, safety and welfare of human subjects, to assure the quality and reliability of the data collected from the study and to provide guidelines for the conduct of clinical research. Information and guidance documents on GCP can be found on the FDA web site [1] and should be studied by the device team well before testing in humans.

8.3 Clinical Research Process

Planning for and running a clinical trial, even a small trial with a non-invasive device, requires considerable effort. Not only must the research questions be determined, there are logistical details including interacting with the IRB, co-ordinating multiple sites if a multi-site trial, collecting an maintaining records, including data records and assuring all principles of human subject safety and ethics are met. If this is your first time, you are strongly encouraged to collaborate with an experienced investigator.

The first step in a clinical study design is to develop the study objective which includes determining the research objective and device claims. The

---

[1] http://goo.gl/IlxxHJ

Clinical Research Steps

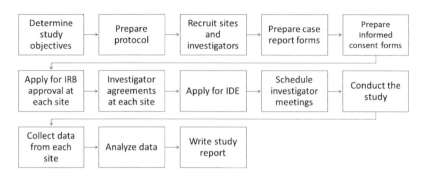

study objective should be phrased as a research question posed to address the proposed medical claims for the device, that is to determine if the device will work for its intended purpose. The research question should specifically address the safety and effectiveness of the given device in a well-defined patient population for one or more outcomes. If the device claims are inadequately known, before engaging in the time and expense of a full clinical trial, conduct a pilot or feasibility study on a small subgroup of patients. The purpose of such a pilot study is to identify claims more precisely, test study procedures, obtain estimates of properties of outcome or other variables and help to determine how many subjects to include in the clinical trial.

The next step is to define the study population and an appropriate clinical control that will lead to an unbiased comparison for the new device. For example, if the new device is a transcatheter heart valve then the control group might be patients receiving a heart valve through traditional open-heart surgery, or might be patients receiving a transcather heart valve that has already received regulatory approval. If the new device is an automated method for determining muscle block during an anesthesia protocol, then the control group is determining block by traditional train-of-four methods, possibly with side-by-side comparison in the same patient.

Study details must be determined, including the clinical, physiological or quality of life parameters to track, the proper sample size so that the study is properly statistically powered and the number of study sites, which is dictated by practical considerations of how many patients each site is likely to recruit and the availability of appropriately trained individuals who can be the local principle investigators for the study. The FDA publishes extensive guidelines on all of these considerations as well as what information from the study should be contained in a final premarket approval report.

IRB approval for the study must be obtained from each site. Important parts of the IRB review and approval process include determining the risks and benefits for research participants, how participants will be recruited and the process of obtaining informed consent from participants. Because each local IRB has different policies and procedures for reviewing and approving research involving human subjects, and because IRB approval can take weeks or months, sufficient time should be allocated for this step. Investigators are advised to review information and forms available on the local IRB web site as soon as possible.

Once the study begins, extensive monitoring functions are required including documenting all adverse events and complete case reports for each subject. The duration and frequency of follow-up information for each subject post-treatment will vary depending on the device being tested and the nature of the study.

8.4 Investigational Device Exemption

For testing new medical devices, an Investigational Device Exemption (IDE) is required before beginning the study. For a significant risk device that presents serious risk to the health safety or welfare of the subject (e.g. a heart valve), IDE approval is required by the local IRB and the FDA. For a nonsignificant risk device (e.g. contact lenses), only local IRB approval is needed before beginning the study. FDA guidance documents can assist in helping you to determine if your device falls in the significant or nonsignificant risk category. The determination of whether a device is nonsignificant risk is made by the local IRB upon application by the investigator.

Some devices proposed for testing in a clinical trial may be exempt from IDE regulations. These include devices already approved for sale if used in accordance with its labeling, and some noninvasive diagnostic devices. The FDA web site has information that can help you to decide if to apply for an IDE-exempt status for your study.

9 Reliability Considerations in Medical Device Development

Mark Hjelle, Heraeus Medical Components

Preparing for the Reliability Challenge

In translating an early-stage medical device prototype from tens to hundreds, thousands and perhaps to millions of units, your product development team has many goals provided to them by investors and internal stakeholders including: reduced unit costs, demonstrated clinical efficacy, the earliest possible forecast for revenue, high production yields and significant quality measures. A common medical product validation threshold is a 95% confidence of a 95% device reliability. Given that validation is the common gateway to clinical studies, eventual market release and revenue, there is necessarily a focus on validation and reliability of the prototypes to be tested on the benchtop, in pre-clinical trials and in human trials. The following table shows the number of device tests that are needed to reach a specific level of reliability with a specific level of confidence.

% Reliability	% Confidence			
	90	95	99	99.9
99.9	2,302	2,995	4,603	6,905
99	114	149	228	688
95	45	59	90	135
90	22	29	44	66

You will notice that there are no values provided in the table for 100% confidence or 100% reliability, and you will notice that the sample sizes needed for 99% intervals and above are generally cost prohibitive. While one can understand that no product can be 100% reliable, to the patient who receives your device that is the reality. For that patient there is no 90%. The device either works or does not. Further, any failure of a Class III medical device could lead to morbidity or mortality. So for the development team a significant and ongoing challenge is device reliability.

The consequences of missing the target on reliability can impact the overall project life or the viability of a whole product line. In other words from a business standpoint, missing reliability goals can result in: 1) missed timelines, 2) delayed clinical start, 3) missed revenue targets prior to market release and potential quality issues in production, 4) reliability issues in the field, 5) warning letters, or 6) field corrective actions.

Example: A search of the FDA's Adverse Event Reporting System (FAERS) or MedWatch for the Teletronics Accufix J-Lead and the Bjork-Shily Heart Valve provides the context for the consequences of poor reliability and the resulting impact to patients. Importantly, one of the greatest challenge that comes from products that have questionable reliability is to balance the risks of product removal vs. the risk of leaving the product in the patient. Historically there has been more patient harm caused by the removal of a potentially "good product" than the removal of a known "bad product." The important point is that once the waters of reliability have been tainted it is hard to balance the fear of the unknown. So the challenge is to address the unknown as soon as possible.

Addressing the Unknown to Find the Sweet Spot

Reliability is a difficult concept to measure and understand because of the time element that drives this topic. In addition, medical device reliability has a historical connotation that large sample sizes and lengthy testing is required to derive the desired results. In the future, with the advancement of computational modeling and rapid prototyping techniques and services, the development of reliability measures for a new product will be easily attainable.

The concept of reliability for medical devices is typically much more than just the relative reliability of an individual product. For example, if the product is an ICD lead, factored reliability at a minimum is influenced by: 1) the lead itself; 2) the implant system, including the ICD, the programmer, software, atrial lead and CRT lead, implant accessories (stylets, introducers) and catheters; 3) the implant procedure including lateral or medial axillary stick, cephalic cutdown, jugular vein, etc; 4) the skills and product knowledge of the implanting physician; and 5) the variability in a given patient's anatomy (both static and dynamic including with high impact activities).

There are items within the control of the product development team as well as reliability issues that are beyond the control of the team. Yet, this should not be considered as a barrier to the team but an opportunity to provide and better device and clinical result for the patient to address the disease state. In the end, this is the desired result for all. Diligent planning and execution of the team during the prototyping and bench testing phases are vital to gain the data and experiences required to understand reliability. These insights will be essential to train and educate the clinical team as to optimal utilization of the medical device/system.

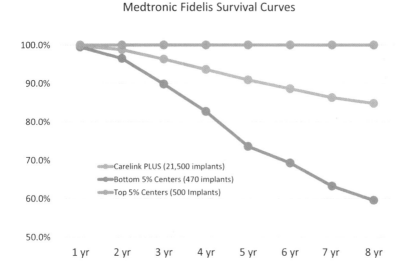

Medtronic Fidelis Survival Curves

The figure above shows available public data from the Medtronic Fidelis performance registry that highlights the challenge and the opportunity for a team seeking to develop an innovative medical device.

The key point of this plotted data, is that the same device yielded clinical survival results in one group of implanters of 100% clinical survival at five years with 335 samples while those from another clinical center had just 73.5% clinical survival at five years with 247 samples.

For each device project team, identification and confirmation of the "sweet spot," as shown in the figure below, is the goal that drives the union of innovation and reliability, that is required to address the unmet needs within the medical device industry.

The consequences of the history of certain ICD and ICD lead failures has been increased scrutiny by regulatory bodies who have required additional, rigorous bench and clinical testing in an effort to prevent future issues. This is not only for the company that had device reliability issue, but all of the players in a given field. This in turn can result in a slowing of innovation within a device area by: 1) increasing internal fears of failure; 2) induced more time for enhanced testing; and 3) increase paperwork to process. All of which means that next generation devices will take longer to reach the market.

The sweet spot is not impossible to achieve as evidenced by numerous examples of products that have found the right reliability and clinical performance, among them being the Medtronic 5076 pacing lead, the St. Jude Tendril pacing lead and the Edwards Sapiens transcatheter heart valve.

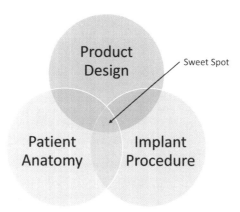

Design and Process Bench Testing Phase to Define Reliability

Once a general framework for the device design is chosen and realized through early prototypes, the next phase can begin with the actual materials and components that will produce the final product. At this point, breaking down the product design into building blocks is recommended. For example, ICD leads have the following building blocks:

- Proximal End: connectors, handles and transition management to the mid-section (body).

- Mid-Section: wire, conductor and lumen management from proximal to distal end.

- Distal Section: electrodes, therapy delivery, flex and shape formation, transition from the mid-section.

Once the building blocks are developed then the task of component testing begins with the use of smart design of experiments (DOE). The smart DOE approach consists of small focused testing to failure, testing in and out of specification experiments that define both the nominal, edge and beyond the edge of specification data: i.e., which will confirm the selected designs for each building block. Key components of a smart DOE plan are:

- Smaller sample sizes : a sequential run of three sets of 10 samples versus one set of 30 samples.

- Sample Selection: DOE software is a useful tool, but all too often the software generates an experiment requiring hundreds of samples. It is acceptable to skip specific samples or reduce the number of samples with thoughtful team input.

- Test to failure: running an experiment with no failures may reveal a poor test set up versus the desired test success: NOTE, do not get lured into a false sense of security with all your tests passing.

- Testing assemblies built wrong: For example if an assembly requires two mechanical crimps, build samples with one crimp. If they pass then the desired two crimps is still valid but now you have both design and process margins.

While testing is being conducted it is important to document any failure modes, for example, document a cohesive versus adhesive bond failure. Knowing *how* a sample failed is of equal importance as to the recorded value of the failure. To optimize reliability testing, one must have a good under-standing of statistics. While there tends to be a fixation on normal data, the world in general is not normal. For example, most joining techniques produce Weibull results so all data distributions should be considered. Consideration should be given to the process capability by measuring or estimating the pro-cess capability index (CpK). Typically, while a high process CpK is considered a good result, it is not the only goal because process capability does not equal reliability. For example, the Takata air bag likely had a very high CpK as is typical for products made by Japanese companies, yet the reliability of the air bag was poor and resulted in injuries and fatalities.

Once quantitative data is obtained, then an effort to develop final computa-tional models of the product is typical next step. The resulting computational models, if properly linked to bench testing, can enable iterative designs (in some cases) to be submitted for regulatory approval without excessive bench testing.

Product Development Process to Deliver Reliability

In general, a good product development process is designed to burn down risks and to manage the risks associated with turning the initial prototypes into full scale production. Again, a focus on reliability can be the difference. A practical product development process can be represented with the follow-ing flow diagram. Items highlighted in green are areas where the focus on device reliability are key outcomes of the activity. For acute products, the ideation and the design and pre-clinical phases each take 3–6 months, while for chronic products, the ideation phase takes 6–9 months and the design and pre-clinical phase takes 6–12 months. The timing for the validation phase cannot be estimated given the variation in types of medical devices.

49

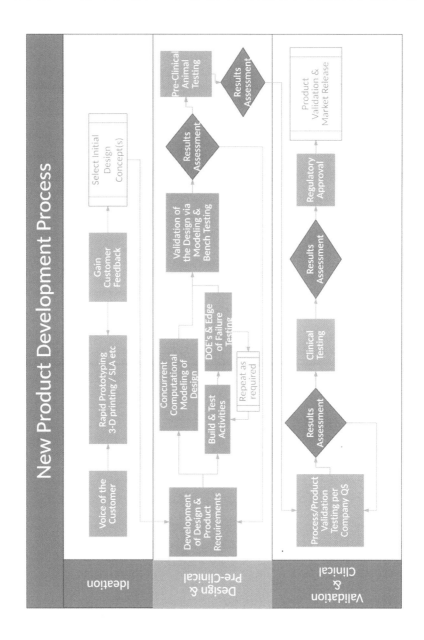

When looking at successes and failures in the recent history of the medical device industry three things stand out:

- The innovation and development of medical devices has brought life changing results to millions of people.

- Companies and projects start with noble intents: failure was not in their plans.

- The products and the innovations that have stood the test of time are reliable in their performance and in their ability to address the unmet clinical needs.

There is an old commercial for an oil filter that simply states the importance of finding the reliability sweet spot. The message was delivered by a mechanic to people who stretched out the intervals between maintenance in order to save money. The mechanic said, "You can pay me now, or you can pay me later." The investment in efforts to reduce risks and develop a reliable product is vital to the success of the overall project and in some cases possibly the company as a whole, particularly for start-ups and mid-size medical device companies.

10 Innovation Notebooks

Paul Iaizzo, University of Minnesota

**You never know when, where, how,
a great new IDEA will hit you!**

Don't forget it! Write it down.

Notebook for Recording Your Ideas

Every innovator should keep a notebook. It should contain a daily log of activities, ideas, sketches and contacts. For example, when you get a business card at a networking event, tape it into your notebook and jot down the context. Review your notebook often, and build on your ideas. If you get in the habit of putting all your sketches and ideas in your notebook, you will know where to find them.

Identification

Table of Contents

Some notebook tips:

- Use a pen or marker for all entries, so that the marks will not smear nor will they be erasable.
- Dont lose it! Put your name on it, a telephone number, email, address and other info on the front cover. Put that same information on the inside front cover, or just tape in your business card.
- Date every entry.
- If your notebook does not have prenumbered pages, number every page.
- At the front include a table of contents: entry date, title of entry, page numbers.
- A notebook with gridded paper aids with figures and sketches.

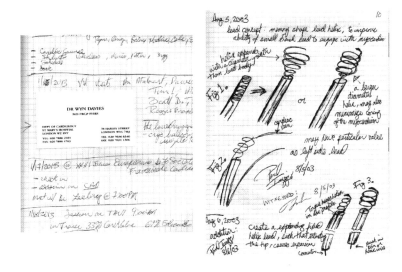

Your sketches do not have to be a da Vinci. Stick figures are your best friend. The important thing is to get your idea down.

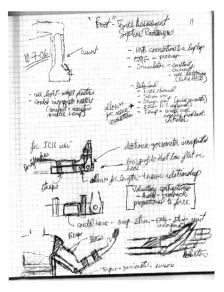

- Try it!
- Practice
- Get a book on sketching
- Take a sketching course
- Enjoy it!

Notebooks and IP Protection

A record of your work that shows and dates the progress of your invention is also important for IP protection. In the U.S., prior to 2013, a record of invention mattered because the U.S. was a first-to-invent country, which meant that whoever had the idea first got the patent. The engineers notebook was one of the ways to determine who that person was.

Today, the U.S. is a first-to-file country like most of the rest of the world. Nevertheless, the notebook is still important for the patenting process. A well-kept notebook will make it easier to communicate with your patent attorney and some patent litigation still makes use of timeline information that is in the engineers notebook.

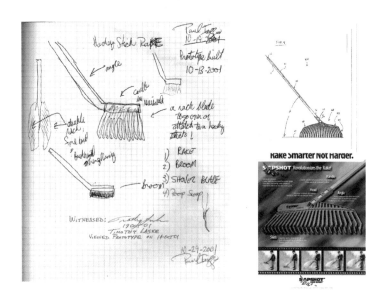

Your Notebook is Valuable

You notebook preserves your rights or those of an employer or academic investigator to your discoveries. It is so important that most companies and some academic labs require that you leave your notebook with the institution when you leave.

Further, a comprehensive notebook enables you, or someone else, to reproduce any part of a methodology completely and accurately, even years later. Every inventor has had the experience of remembering that five years ago they had a circuit or code snippet or mechanical component that performed a function needed now, and has also experienced either the joy of digging back into a notebook to find the old idea or the frustration of having lost the notebook so that the old idea was gone forever.

11 Patent Basics

William Durfee, University of Minnesota

Disclaimer   This chapter provides information about patent practice and patent law. The content of this chapter is intended as general information only, and is not to be interpreted as legal advice. For questions and guidance about a specific situation, you should consult a patent attorney or patent agent.

Intellectual Property

- IP is essential to med tech development
- Forms of IP
  - Technology disclosure
  - Provisional patent
  - Patent application
  - Issued patent

Friday, April 22, 2005
Medtronic will pay $1.35 billion to settle patent lawsuit
Memphis Business Journal

Jury rules against Boston Scientific in drug-coated stent patent lawsuit
By Barnaby J. Feder   Published: February 17, 2008

Bloomberg
Abbott Wins Reversal of J&J's $1.67 Billion Patent Victory
February 23, 2011, 4:34 PM EST

The cost of Medtronic's battle with Edwards Lifesciences over TAVI: $245M, so far
November 20, 2012 11:48 am by Arundhoti Parmar | 0 Comments

October 22, 2012 1:40 a.m. ET
Volcano Shares Rise After Patent Win Over St. Jude Medical

The value of company is in its intellectual property and in the ability of staff to generate IP, not in the products. When you make your pitch to VCs or potential business partners, they will take a careful look at your IP when considering the value of the deal.

Because patents are so valuable in med tech, it is critical that intellectual property be considered early in the innovation process. Three issues are paramount:

1. Can my idea be patented?
2. Does my idea infringe upon existing patents?

3. Who owns my idea?

What is a Patent?

Patents

- Grants the inventor a limited use monopoly
- Grants inventor the right to exclude others from making, using or selling the invention
- Only valid in the issuing country
- Protection is described in the claims
- Must be
  1. New
  2. Useful
  3. Non-obvious

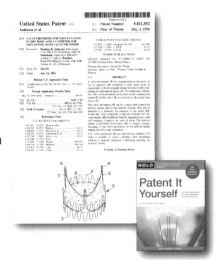

A patent is the grant of a property right to an inventor, which in return for the inventor publicly disclosing the invention gives the inventor a limited term monopoly to practice the invention. Normally, the term of a patent is 20 years from the filing date. In the U.S. patents are issued by the United States Patent and Trademark Office. In the words of the U.S. patent law, what is granted is "the right to exclude others from making, using, offering for sale, or selling" the invention in the U.S.

What is important to recognize is that the right is to exclude others from practicing the invention so it is up to the inventor to enforce the patent. A patents gives you the right to sue another company whose product infringes on your patent. However, lawsuits are generally expensive, and the other company will most likely counter with a suit contending that your patent is invalid and never should have been issued. This is one reason why your patent must have strong claims and is why you should have a patent attorney write your patent to protect your invention properly.

There are three types of patents: utility, design and plant. This chapter will focus on utility patents, which are for a new and useful process, machine, article of manufacture or composition of matter. This is the category that covers all medical devices, although sometimes a company will protect an invention through a design patent along with a utility patent.

When Did U.S. Patents Start?

Patents have been part of the United States from the beginning. Article 1, Section 8 of the U.S. constitution specifies the powers of Congress and includes this language:

> "To promote the Progress of Science and useful Arts, by securing for limited Times to Authors and Inventors the exclusive Right to their respective Writings and Discoveries"

Congress passed the first patent law in 1790. The most significant recent patent law is the America Invents Act, which was signed into law in 2011.

Patents are only valid in the issuing country. A company will assess which markets it wants to sell in and will file for patents only in those countries.

An Invention is Patentable if it is New, Useful and Non-Obvious

New   Your invention must be new for it to be patented. "New" means it has not been described in any printed publication (books, magazines, journals), has not been described in an issued patent or published patent application, and has not been in public use and has not been available to or known by the public before the filing date of your patent. This is why searching the patent data base is so important because your invention may already be described in an earlier patent.

Non-Obvious   Along with being new, your invention must be a non-obvious improvement over the prior art. For this, your invention is compared to the prior art (all relevant patents and other knowledge) and a determination is made on whether your idea would have been obvious "to a person having ordinary skill in the art," which means a person familiar with the technology area related to the invention.

For a simple example, suppose plastic coffee cups were around in every color but red. You come up with the idea of a red cup. Your idea would be novel (passes the "new" test for patentability), but would not pass the non-obvious test because it would be obvious to come up with another color cup.

Determining whether an idea is obvious can be difficult and is almost always at the core of arguing with the patent office over whether your idea should receive a patent, and is almost always at the core of litigation over whether an issued patent is valid. For example, when you file a patent, the examiner may immediately reject the application because the idea is described in an earlier patent that failed to come up in your initial search. More than likely, however, the examiner will reject the application based on the combination of two or more patents viewed together, making the argument that if someone like you had those two patents in front of them, coming up with your idea would be obvious. Now it is up to you to argue back that no, even given the two pieces of prior art, your idea is unique, creative and non-obvious.

Useful   This is the easy one, because if your invention works or could work, then it is useful, even if someone else thinks your invention is silly. A perpetual motion machine or other inventions that violate a fundamental law of physics would fail this test because it could never be made to work, which means it is not useful.

Provisional Patent Applications

A provisional patent application is low-cost first filing that can provide some protection to the inventor by establishing an early filing date. The inventor then has up to 12 months to file a utility (nonprovisional) patent on the same invention and can claim as an effective filing date the date the provisional was filed. Claims are not included in a provisional application, but the provisional must have text and drawings that describe how to make and use the invention in sufficient detail to support the claims that might be made in the later utility application. Provisional patents are not evaluated or even looked at by the patent office. If after 12 months you have not filed the nonprovisional, the provisional is considered abandoned, and it is as if nothing happened because it is never published or posted on a database that your competitors can search.

Plain language can be used in a provisional application, the drawings can be informal and the document can be short. You can even file a technical article as a provisional application, but first make sure that the article fully describes how to make and use the invention, which often is not the case for academic journal or conference papers.

The common flaw with a provisional is that shortly after filing you make an important improvement to your idea that is not described in the provisional. This means in the regular patent application that has claims covering those improvements, you cannot claim the early filing date of the provisional, which defeats its purpose.

Generally, you should make your provisional application look as much like a regular application as you can, including background, summary of the invention, description of the drawings and a detailed description of the invention. A good practice is to draft some initial claims for the invention before writing the provisional. While the claims are not included in the provisional, you can use them to check that the description is adequate to fully support the claims.

Effective Filing Date

The "effective filing date" (also called the priority date) is important in the world of patents. For example, if your invention was
disclosed or known before that date than you cannot receive
a patent for the invention. Another reason the effective filing
date is important is that if you and someone else independently
made the same invention and both you and the other person
filed for a patent, the first one to file would get the patent [1]

One benefit of filing a provisional patent application is that
if you file the follow-on utility patent within 12 months of the
provisional, your effective filing date is the date that you filed the
provisional application. In a fast-moving field, this earlier filing
date can give you a jump on your competition in the who-filed-
first race. At the same time, the 20 year protection provided by
a patent still starts on the date that the utility patent was filed.

Along with the provisional patent application case, the effective filing date of a utility application may be that of an earlier
application where continuation applications or international applications are involved. This is where consulting a patent attorney is important.

"Patent Pending"

You can claim "Patent Pending" for your invention once you
have filed a patent application, and until the patent prosecution has finished. If the patent is issued, then you can switch to
claim that the invention is patented. You can also claim "Patent
Pending" for the 12 months after filing a provisional patent application.

Disclosure

Disclosing your invention publicly has ramifications for patenting. Ways that
you can disclose include, but are not limited to:

- Published journal or conference paper
- Bringing to a trade show
- Describing in a presentation that is open to the public (which includes
  most department seminars at a university)
- Posting a YouTube video
- Displaying on your lab web site
- Showing to a company without having a nondisclosure agreement
- Showing at an undergraduate capstone design show

- Discussing with colleagues outside your organization
- The automatic publication of a patent application that occurs 18 months after filing

But, keeping the invention to yourself sometimes is not the best strategy. You might want to show your idea to a company that might be interested in licensing or buying your invention. If you are an academic, you might want to describe your idea in a journal article, or at a conference or in a research proposal, all of which are important for academic recognition. Keep in mind that submitting a conference or journal article that describes the idea does not constitute disclosure. Because the review process is confidential, disclosure only happens when the article is accepted and published. The same is true with a research proposal because the proposal review process is confidential and reviewers are obligated not to disclose what they learn from reading your proposal.

There are two ways you can protect yourself when you want talk about your idea to others. The first is to ask a company or the people you are meeting with to sign a nondisclosure agreement (NDA). Simple NDAs are available from your organization or online (see `www.nolo.com`.

The second is to file a provisional patent application (or a regular utility application). If you are at a university, contact your technology transfer office about filing a provisional if you are close to submitting a journal or conference paper on your idea. Once the provisional is filed, then you can disclose your idea and be protected.

If you intentionally or unintentionally disclose your idea before filing, you still may have 12 months to file a patent in the U.S., but you will have lost your rights to file a patent in any other country.

Bottom Line on Disclosing

Do not disclose your idea to others unless an NDA is in place or unless you have filed a provisional or utility application.

Parts of a Patent Application

Along with various forms and fees, a patent application consists of the the specification and one or more drawings.

The specification must have these sections

Title A title for the invention.

Related Applications A list of any related applications, for example the provisional patent application if a provisional was filed.

Background A few paragraphs where you describe the field of the invention and a few key pieces of prior art to highlight how the prior art is different from your invention and to show what improvements are needed over the prior art.

Summary A brief description of your invention focusing how it is an improvement over the prior art and how it solves some of the problems with the prior art that you describe in the background section.

Description of Drawings A one sentence description of each drawing.

Description of the Invention Typically the longest part of the patent, this section must completely and accurately describe the invention. Each feature in each drawing must be explained. Variations (embodiments) of the basic idea are described. Terms are defined as needed, which can impact how claims are interpreted. Often the description has two parts with the first describing the invention and the second describing how to use the invention. The examples of various embodiments and ways of using the invention are meant to illustrate, but not limit the scope of the invention.

Claims The claims are the most important part of the patent because they state exactly what is protected. While the specification is broad and can describe many aspects of the invention, the claims are specific and exact. Each claim is one sentence and contains a number of elements that state the essential features of the invention. Some claims may be dependent, which means they add additional elements to the independent claim they depend upon. The patent examiner compares the claims in the application against the prior art to determine if the claim should be allowed. For patents that have issued, the claims are used to determine whether another device infringes on your patent.

Abstract A brief summary of the specification

The application must have one or more drawings that explain the invention. The drawings are in a particular format and must be quite clear in showing the invention.

Patent Search

The U.S. and foreign patent literature is an invaluable resource for getting ideas and also the place to go to determine if your concept is unique and patentable. Patents are an excellent source of information about a complex med tech product because the description of the invention in a patent must be sufficiently detailed to allow another to build the invention. Although comprehensive searches are best done by professionals, inventors are fully capable of doing a capable and competent job searching the patent literature.

A patentability search is a search of current and expired patents, as well as of books, articles and other publications to determine if your invention is new and nonobvious compared to the prior art. A validity search is used after a patent is issued and one company sues another for infringement. The company being sued will do an exhaustive search to see if the patent office missed a piece of prior art when determining that the issued patent was valid[2].

Search Strategy

Here is a suggested strategy for conducting a search.

1. Determine the likely classification(s) of your invention by coming up with the key terms that describe the invention. Patents are cataloged using the Cooperative Patent Classification (CPC) scheme[3], which includes classes and subclasses.

2. Once you have likely CPC classes and subclasses, pull all of the patents in those categories to review. You will likely have to narrow your classification as broad classes can have tens of thousands of patents, which is generally too much to review.

3. Determine which of the patents found in the step above are relevant by looking at the title, abstract and front-page drawing. This first screening must be quick as you may have hundreds of patents to look at.

4. Review published (but not issued) patent applications in the same categories.

5. For those patents passing your screen, do an in-depth review of the drawings, specification and claims.

6. For the highly relevant patents you find, look at the References Cited section of the patent to find other relevant patents. You can also use the search engine to do a reverse citation search. That is, if Patent A is one of the relevant patents you found, you can search for all of the patents issued after Patent A that cite Patent A.

7. Finally, search by keyword. While keyword searches are easy, they can miss many relevant patents.

---

[2]One consequence of suing another company for infringement is that the litigation may result in your patent being declared invalid, which is a risk you must take when initiating an infringement lawsuit.

[3]In 2015, the CPC replaced the U.S. Patent Classification (USPC).

Why Keyword-Only Searches Don't Work

Searching by key word will miss important patents because patents are intentionally written to be as broad as possible. For example, it is impossible to find patents covering the brake on the Oxo Salad Spinner by typing "salad spinner" into a patent search engine. The reason is that the title of U.S. patent 6,018,883 is "Brake for Device for Drying Foods," because the inventors did want to limit their invention to only cover spinning a salad.

Publication of Patent Applications

Your patent application will be published 18 months after it is filed, or 18 months after the provisional was filed if the nonprovisional application is claiming an effective filing date of the provisional. The application is published no matter where things stand in the patent prosecution process. What this means is that no matter what, your invention becomes public 18 months after filing the patent, even if you never get the patent. When searching for patents, you can tell an entry is a published application by the format of its number, which will be something like US20110064858 A1, compared to an issued patent that will have a number like US8778436 B2. To further confuse matters, applications also have an application number, which will be something like US 12/804,032.

Suggested Online Patent Search Engines

USPTO `www.uspto.gov/patents-application-process/search-patents` (issued and published patents)

Google `patents.google.com` (excellent for U.S. and foreign patents)

FreePatentsOnline `www.freepatentsonline.com/search.html` (good for US or EP searching)

Patent Process

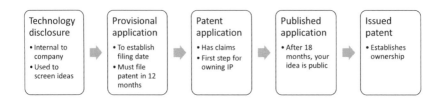

Be clear on the form of your IP. A technology disclosure is an internal company process where an employee discloses a new invention for the company to evaluate. A provisional patent application establishes an invention priority date and is simple to do, but is not evaluated for validity. A patent application is the first step towards protecting invention rights. An issued patent (U.S. or non-U.S.) is the only form of IP that has been fully evaluated for validity and the only form of IP that can be used to protect your invention. Most inventions never make it to the stage of an issued patent.

Patent Costs

The following table shows the approximate fees to have an attorney prepare a patent application

WHAT	FEE (USD)
Provisional application	1,500
Utility, simple (paper clip)	6,000
Utility, minimal (umbrella)	8,000
Utility, complex (MRI)	15,000 +

The next table shows the USPTO filing fees in USD.

WHAT	FEE	MICRO ENTITY FEE
Provisional	260	65
Utility	1,600	400
Issue fee	960	240
Maintenance, 3.5 yrs	1,600	400
Maintenance, 7.5 yrs	3,600	900
Maintenance, 11.5 yrs	7,400	1,850

More Information

Books

Pressman and Tuytschaevers, *Patent It Yourself*, Nolo Press.
Pressman and Stim, *Patent Pending in 24 Hours*, Nolo Press.
Pressman and Stim, *Patents for Beginners*, Nolo Press.
Hitchcock, *Patent Searching Made Easy*, Nolo Press.
Lo and Pressman, *How to Make Patent Drawings*, Nolo Press.

Pressman, *Patent It Yourself*, Nolo Press, is an excellent guide to patents. While a do-it-yourself patent is not recommended, having a familiarity with the patent process is helpful when deciding whether to pursue a patent and when interacting with your patent attorney.

Websites

USPTO www.uspto.gov/
Bitlaw http://www.bitlaw.com/

12 Intellectual Property Strategy for the Early Stage Medical Device Business

David Black, Schwegman Lundberg & Woessner, P.A.

IP Assets as a Business Value

For many medical device businesses, a substantial portion of the business value is represented by the intellectual property assets. A prudent IP strategy provides that these assets are properly recognized, well-protected, and judiciously deployed for the benefit of the shareholders. This chapter describes elements of a typical IP strategy, and for your particular early stage medical device technology company, these recommendation must be adjusted to align with your business objectives for growth, available budget, resources, and timeline.

A robust IP portfolio will include a balanced mix of copyrights, trademarks, trade secrets, agreements, and patent assets. For example, corporate documents, agreements, advertising, marketing and other such material are probably eligible for copyright protection. Copyright protection is very low cost and is to be viewed as low-hanging fruit for capture. Material that provides a competitive advantage if maintained in secrecy is likely to be a suitable candidate for trade secret protection. Trade secret material can be protected by a schedule of protection measures for preventing discovery by unauthorized personnel. A patent can be viewed as the opposite end of the spectrum from a trade secret; the patent application is laid open to the public.

You will need patent counsel input to help develop and deploy your IP strategy. Counsel will be able to help you select those innovations suited for trade secret protection or patent protection, select marks for trademark protection, and select materials for copyright protection.

For those innovations earmarked for patent protection, good counsel can also assist in developing a filing plan, provide guidance on subject matter for inclusion, and write claims consistent with the IP strategy. In particular, changes in the law, the regulatory framework, business strategy, resources, competitive pressures, and many other factors will play an important role in making choices consistent with a comprehensive intellectual property strategy.

To preserve capital and build an IP portfolio in a cost-effective manner, an early stage company should concentrate on a blended approach including domestically filed patent and trademark applications, carefully selected international filings, selective use of freedom to operate analysis, leveraged post-grant review opportunities, and thoughtful controls on the rate of prosecution.

Patent Timeline

A typical patent application timeline is illustrated in the figure above. Before filing a patent application, a search of the relevant art should be conducted either by the company or by a patent attorney. The figure illustrates filing a United States provisional application at time 0 months. The application should reflect the findings of the search. At a time no later than 12 months thereafter, a non-provisional application is filed. In due course, the US patent office will conduct their own search and examination and provide feedback in a document known as an Office action. To advance prosecution, the applicant is required to respond to each Office action with a written response. The example illustrates two such cycles followed by a notice of allowance and then grant. A typical duration for the illustrated process is several years.

The next figure illustrates an international application filing timeline. Here, the applicant has filed an application under the terms of the Patent Cooperation Treaty (PCT) no later than 12 months after the US provisional application filing date. The PCT application is processed in accordance with rules of the World Intellectual Property Organization and following this proceeding, the example applicant has filed national phase filings in four countries (or regions). Each national phase filing proceeds much like that at the US in terms of Office actions and responses. Notably, a PCT application does not, in and of itself, result in a PCT patent or an international patent.

An investor in the new business will be interested in reviewing any patents held by the company. Investors often use the IP portfolio as a proxy for business value. Sophisticated investors understand that a pending provisional application is better than a back-of-the-napkin idea but not as impressive as a comprehensive portfolio of several patents, or even just one patent. Investor confidence will increase as the IP portfolio matures. Patent office validation of the core innovation inspires investor confidence. Patents also can help trigger buying decisions by customers, attract business partners, and attract qualified employees. The relationship between portfolio maturity and cost (or value) can be represented by the graph shown in the figure below.

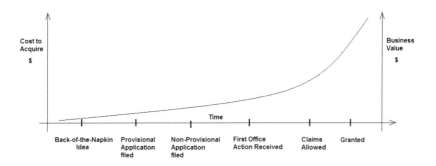

With this understanding, it makes sense to allocate resources to aggressively develop a patent portfolio. Various tactics can be employed to accomplish this. For example, a patent applicant can leverage the opportunity to control the pace of the patent application prosecution timeline (between the filing date of the application and grant date of the patent). The US Patent and Trademark Office offers several tools to accelerate the application process. For example, an applicant can pay a fee and request expedited processing and expect final determination of allowance or rejection in under 12 months. Other options are available for advancing the application to the front of the prosecution queue. For example, favorable treatment of a similar application in a first country can be leveraged to expedite prosecution in a second country.

For some businesses, rather than accelerating, it may make sense to reduce the rate of prosecution. For example, patent applications directed to certain software technologies are currently struggling with patent office guidelines that may deny grant of a patent. By inserting a delay in the prosecution, the applicant may be able to shift the timeline to a period where a more favorable review is possible. For these technologies, it may make sense to leverage opportunities to slow the rate of prosecution. Tactics here can include filing a PCT application, filing an appeal to the Board of Patent Appeals and Interferences (PTAB), filing a provisional application, withholding payment of official fees at time of filing an application, and buying extensions to allow filing of a delayed response.

Experienced patentees also recognize that prosecution time and cost is related to claim breadth. In other words, a broad claim will be examined relative to a larger body of prior art and a narrow claim will be examined relative to a smaller body of prior art. Overly broad claims can drive costs during prosecution and later, when the patent is asserted, broad claims may leave a competitor with a viable defense against a charge of infringement. Right-sized claims have the proper breadth, are not excessively costly to prosecute, and when granted, are fully defensible. Keep in mind that a continuation application can be filed to incrementally acquire broader overall coverage.

IP Landscape Audits

As the company grows, it may be valuable to conduct periodic IP audits. An audit can reveal findings that can provide feedback for the IP strategy. An IP audit can reveal flaws in ownership records for patent assets, identify those patent assets worthy of further maintenance fee payments, identify those applications that should be abandoned, and identify those IP assets that are well-suited for disposition via licensing, donation, or as part of a tax strategy. An IP audit can also include a critical review of agreements, licenses and joint ventures and ensure that ongoing obligations are being met. Most importantly, an audit should include a review of the current offerings of commercial products and services and evaluate alignment between these offerings and the IP portfolio.

The company should be ever vigilant for imminent disclosures of new products and innovations because a sale event or a disclosure before having filed an application can impair or preclude patentability. Ensure that any innovation likely to arise in the course of the disclosure is either already patented or ensure that a corresponding patent application is already pending. Disclosures can take the form of an exhibit at an industry conference, a press release, or a published manuscript. The scope of the disclosure should be reviewed carefully relative to currently-filed patent applications.

Strategy for IP Filing

The med tech company should develop a balanced plan for filing both offensive patent applications and defensive patent applications. A defensive patent application can ensure that others are unable to block core activities of your business. An offensive patent application can erect a barrier to exclude a competitor from accessing technology of interest to your business. An offensive patent can cover technology that may be in a related field or cover ideas that are not seen as core to the company business. A patent can be viewed as a bargaining chip that can be licensed to others or asserted as counter-measures in the event the company is the target of an infringement challenge.

A sophisticated patent strategy can include filing applications in areas selected to anticipate the business goals of the competition. Insightful analytics and trend analysis can help the company identify the development direction of the competition. Resources dedicated to developing solutions in these areas can pay dividends when the competition discovers that your company already has patents in place.

Budgeting resources for development of the patent portfolio is essential. This entails forecasting company growth rates and patent application filing plans. Set a reasonable budget for each patent application at the outset, but as technologies are developed, and at the time of deciding to file a patent application, ascribe a value to the subject technology and make budget adjustments accordingly. If, on the other hand, the company allocates a fixed budget to each patent application without discriminating as to relative value, then some matters will be over-funded and others under-funded.

The company should create a documented program by which patent application decisions are made. For example, the program can establish a patent review board and include guidelines for uncovering innovations and selecting those suitable for patenting. The members of the review board should include patent counsel and include folks from marketing and from research and development.

To meet a filing target, the company should proactively encourage all employees to come forward with clever innovations. For example, in the product development process, the company should conduct blue-sky brainstorming sessions in which all ideas are unconditionally supported. The results of a brainstorming session can be evaluated according to the company's IP strategy; some ideas will be suited for trade secret treatment and others are likely candidates for patenting.

Foreign patent protection is generally costly. For many early stage medical device companies, the prudent course entails filing primarily in the United States, and filing internationally for only a small number of innovations. Those innovations having the greatest promise for licensing or the best prospects for blocking a competitor should be carefully chosen and earmarked for a foreign patent application. A variety of international filing strategies are available but for many innovations, a PCT filing provides a reasonable gateway to later national phase filings.

The company should watch for opportunities to file a design patent application. A design patent is directed to ornamental aspects of an innovation rather than functional aspects. Prosecution is rather quick, the patent term is shorter than that of a utility patent, and there are no maintenance fees.

The company should ensure that existing opinions of counsel are properly maintained and updated as appropriate. Importantly, the company must ensure that the commercial products are consistent with the advice of counsel as to a freedom to operate opinion. For commercial offerings that are not already covered by an opinion of counsel, the company should carefully consider the merits of evaluating and obtaining an opinion.

The low-cost opportunities presented by US post-grant procedures can be leveraged. For example, the company can consider clearing troublesome patents using the *inter partes* review mechanism. In addition, the company can monitor the *inter partes* challenges lodged against competitors and adjust course accordingly. This can include bolstering IP rights with an eye towards discouraging third party challenges.

Growing a successful company in the medical device space is complex. The nascent company should strive to create a business culture that nurtures genuine respect for all intellectual property. This involves educating all employees regarding the fundamental principles of intellectual property.

The smart company, in coordination with advice from competent legal counsel, will leverage its IP opportunities to ensure its success and longevity. Further, the smart company will periodically review its IP strategy and routinely adjust the strategy to reflect changes in the business climate, growth plans for the business, changes in the law, and changes in the technology.

13 Regulatory

Paul Iaizzo and William Durfee, , University of Minnesota

13.1 Defining 'Medical Device'

What is a "Medical Device"

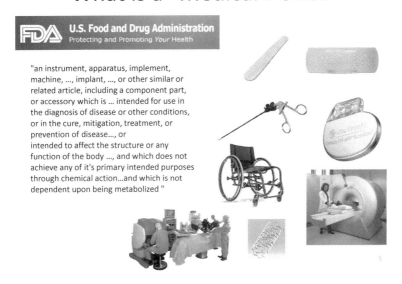

Before looking regulations, 'medical device' must be defined. Medical devices are exceptionally broad, and include everything from a bandage to a robot surgery system.

In the U.S., regulation of medical devices is done by the Center for Devices and Radiological Health (CDRH), a division of the Food and Drug Administration (FDA). Use the FDA site (`http://www.fda.gov/MedicalDevices`) to help you get started on medical devices and their regulation.

The FDA definition of a medical device is:

"an instrument, apparatus, implement, machine, contrivance, implant, in vitro reagent, or other similar or related article, including a component part, or accessory which is:

- recognized in the official National Formulary, or the United States Pharmacopoeia, or any supplement to them,
- intended for use in the diagnosis of disease or other conditions, or in the cure, mitigation, treatment, or prevention of disease, in man or other animals, or
- intended to affect the structure or any function of the body of man or other animals, and which does not achieve any of its primary intended purposes through chemical action within or on the body of man or other animals and which is not dependent upon being metabolized for the achievement of any of its primary intended purposes."

13.2 Medical Device Class

The FDA divides medical devices into three categories depending on risk

Class I: Low Risk Bandages and crutches.
Class II: Intermediate Risk Power wheelchairs, guide wires and stents.
Class III: High Risk Drug delivery pumps, heart valves and deep brain stimulators. Typically life sustaining devices.

One part of the FDA site (`http://goo.gl/ryjJk`) guides you in how to determine if your device is Class I, II, III. Follow the links and find the name of your device. The description of the device will include the classification.

For example, from the Device Classification Panels page (`http://goo.gl/L811G`), Part 870 Cardiovascular → Subpart D Cardiovascular Prosthetic Devices → 870.3925 Replacement heart valve, takes you to the page (`http://goo.gl/e068y`), where you can find out that a replacement heart valve is a Class III device that requires premarket approval.

13.3 Regulatory Approval

Regulatory Boards Require

Evidence to support claims that a technology is safe (Europe), or safe and effective (U.S.)

Class I Devices

Most Class I (low risk) devices fall in the FDA's exempt category, which means FDA clearance is not required for marketing. For example, new tongue depressor does not require FDA approval. However, even if exempt, Class I devices must still be registered with the FDA and must follow the "general controls" established by the FDA, which among other things establish manufacturing standards and labeling requirements that must be followed.

Class II Devices

Many Class II (moderate risk) devices can use the 510(k) pathway for approval. Here the manufacturer must demonstrate that the new device is "substantially equivalent" to a predicate device that is already on the market. The concept is that if there is a device already being sold that has FDA approval, there is no need for the new device to independently prove that it is safe and effective.

To receive approval (called a "clearance") under 510(k) the new device is compared to the predicate device using the following questions:

1. Has the predicate device been cleared under the 510(k) process?
2. Do the new device and the predicate device have the same intended use?
3. Do the two devices have similar technical characteristics?
4. If the technical characteristics are different, do the new features raise questions of safety and effectiveness and has data been provided that the new device is at least as safe and effective as the predicate device?

In making its substantially equivalent case, the applicant typically relies on data from bench testing and animal testing. Some devices can prove equivalence just from careful bench tests. Human testing is rarely needed and when requested by the FDA generally involve clinical studies with a small number of patients.

If the FDA agrees with the applicant that the new device is equivalent to the predicate, it will issue a Substantially Equivalent (SE) letter. If not it will issue a Not Substantially Equivalent (NSE) letter and the device will then be automatically placed in Class III.

Class III Devices

Class III devices go through the pre-market approval (PMA) process, which requires demonstrating that the new device is safe and effective in humans. A PMA requires substantial and costly clinical trials in human subjects.

Investigational Device Exemption

In order to enable research studies using human testing before the device is approved through the 510(k) or PMA process, investigators apply for an investigational device exemption (IDE). A non-significant risk device can be approved for research use by the local institutional review board (IRB). A significant risk device must be approved by the IRB and by the FDA.

In Europe

To obtain CE mark prior to marketing a device in Europe, the regulatory process is primarily about safety, letting the market determine whether the device is effective.

Regulatory Process is Significant

FDA Submission is Complex

Courtesy of Alex Hill,
Medtronic

This stack is one copy of a corporate submission to the FDA for pre-market approval. It exemplifies the complexity and effort required for approval of a new Class III medical device.

14 Reimbursement Basics

Michael Finch, Childrens Hospitals and Clinics

> Reimbursement requires evidence to support claims that a technology leads to better patient outcomes at lower cost than existing solutions

14.1 Introduction to Reimbursement

Reimbursement by third-party payers is a separate process from regulatory approval, although without approval there will be no reimbursement. Reimbursement is a higher bar than approval because along with proving that your device is safe and effective, you must prove that your device is cost-effective. For example, approval for reimbursement almost always requires publication of research studies in peer reviewed journals as the evidence supporting your claims about your device.

Reimbursement is essential because no patient pays for a medical device out-of-pocket but rather the cost is paid by a insurance company. Without reimbursement, the business model for your new device is not likely to be viable. Understanding the reimbursement process is complex and specialists are often hired to take the company through the reimbursement maze.

To start at the very beginning, third party payers are entities or organizations that pay for some or all of a person's medical expenses. Government reimbursement programs include Medicare, Medicaid, TRICARE/ CHAMPUS, and the Veterans Health Administration and Workers Compensation. Commercial or private insurance plans include Blue Cross/ Blue Shield, Prudential, Aetna, Cigna, United. WellPoint) and managed care organizations such as Kaiser, GroupHealth Cooperative and HealthPartners.

When it comes to developing a reimbursement strategy for your device, focus your time and attention on the two most powerful and influential types of third party payers in the US: the Centers for Medicare and Medicaid Services (CMS), who oversee Medicare and Medicaid, and private (commercial) payers.

Providers are those persons, institutions, facilities and firms who are eligible to provide services and supplies. Examples of providers include:

- hospitals of all types (i.e., acute care, rehab, psych, long term, specialty)
- skilled nursing facilities
- intermediate care facilities
- home health agencies
- physicians
- independent diagnostic laboratories
- independent facilities providing x-ray services
- outpatient physical, occupational, and speech pathology services
- ambulance companies
- chiropractors
- facilities providing kidney dialysis or transplant services

The reimbursement catechism says that reimbursement is a three legged stool consisting of coverage, coding and payment as shown in the following figure.

Some Definitions

Coverage The processes and criteria used to determine whether a product, service, or procedure will be reimbursed.

Coding Numeric and alpha-numeric symbols that describe the procedure performed and reason why it was performed. Used by hospitals and physicians to submit bills to insurers. Used by payers to research healthcare utilization.

Payment Dollar amount reimbursed based on a specific methodology. The specific methodology varies based on type of payer and policy decisions.

A provider, which can be an institution (such as a hospital) or a person (for instance a physician), provides some service to a patient. It may be as simple as seeing the patient in the clinic or as complex as a surgery. It may be prescribing a drug or providing diabetic education. The provider determines what services they provided, attach an appropriate code to each service and transmit these, in the form of a bill, to the third party payer.

The third party payer first checks to see if each of the services provided is a "covered service". This is not as simple as it may sound because which services are covered and which are not varies by payer and by the specific insurance plan. Typically, payers cover services they consider "medically necessary" and deny services and technologies that are deemed "experimental and investigational". But the definition of "medically necessary" and "experimental or investigational" varies by payer.

If the payer determines the service is not covered, the provider receives no payment for the service. If it is covered, the third party payer next determines how much it will pay for the service and passes the amount on to the provider. This is not a straight forward process as different payers use different methodologies.

In the remainder of this chapter we will discuss each leg of the stool in more detail starting with coverage, then coding then reimbursement.

14.2 Coverage

For coverage, insurance companies want the evidence of clinical benefit, cost and utilization to come from peer-reviewed articles in credible medical journals, a review of available studies on a particular topic, evidence-based consensus statements by practitioner organizations, expert opinions of health care professionals and guidelines from nationally recognized health care organizations. In short, they are looking for evidence and not just the company saying the product is wonderful.

More to the point, insurance companies are looking for:

- Final approval from the appropriate government regulatory bodies.
- Scientific evidence that supports conclusions concerning the effectiveness of the technology on health outcomes.
- Technology that improves the net health outcome.
- Technology that is as beneficial as established alternatives.
- Improvement that is attainable not just in experimental and investigational settings.
- Evidence that the new technology is better than the current standard of care.
- Credible estimates of the cost of the new approach compared to the current practice and evidence that any extra cost is justified by the gain in quality or clinical outcomes.
- Consensus on when the new treatment be used, including patient selection criteria.

Medicare

The most powerful and influential entity in the coverage process is Medicare. Given the size and scope of Medicare, the coverage process is often critical to the survival of a new technology. More often than not, commercial insurers follow Medicare's lead in developing their coverage polices. If Medicare does not cover a new technology, it will be an uphill effort to obtain coverage from commercial payors.

In order for Medicare to cover and pay for an item or service, it must be medically necessary and meet the reasonable and necessary" requirement "... the Social Security Act provides that Medicare may not pay for expenses of items and services that are not reasonable and necessary for the diagnosis and treatment of illness or injury or to improve the functioning of a malformed body member. § 1862(a)(1)(A)."

The American Medical Association Model Managed Care Contract, frequently accepted by commercial insurers, suggests the following definition of medically necessary: "Health care services or procedures that a prudent physician would provide to a patient for the purpose of preventing, diagnosing or treating an illness, injury, disease or its symptoms in a manner that is (a) in accordance with generally accepted standards of medical practice; (b) clinically appropriate in terms of type, frequency, extent, site and duration; and (c) not primarily for the economic benefit of the health plans and purchasers or for the convenience of the patient, treating physician or other health care provider."

Medicare coverage decisions can be either nationwide (NCD) or local (LCD). (For reference, only about 20-30 national coverage decisions are made each year). To find if a service is covered by Medicare go to the CMS.gov indexes. [1] NCDs, which are updated in real time, and LCD, which are updated weekly, provide information on numerous Medicare covered and not covered services and procedures.

Medicare will often deny coverage to new technologies because the research is lacking, inconsistent or insufficiently persuasive. Transcutaneous Electrical Nerve Stimulation (TENS) for Chronic Low Back Pain is an example. Those attempting to garner Medicare coverage are advised to review the Medicare's solution to this interesting case at the CMS site. [2] In this case Medicare responded: "TENS is not reasonable and necessary for the treatment of CLBP under section 1862(a)(1)(A) of the Act."

However, in their own words, "In order to support additional research on the use of TENS for CLBP, we will cover this item under section 1862(a)(1)(E) of the Social Security Act (the Act) subject to all of the following conditions:

1. Coverage under this section expires three years after the publication of this decision on the CMS website.

---

[1] http://goo.gl/61XWbV
[2] http://goo.gl/Hm18o7

2. The beneficiary is enrolled in an approved clinical study meeting all of the requirements below. The study must address one or more aspects of the following questions in a randomized, controlled design using validated and reliable instruments. This can include randomized crossover designs when the impact of prior TENS use is appropriately accounted for in the study protocol.

    a) Does the use of TENS provide clinically meaningful reduction in pain in Medicare beneficiaries with CLBP?

    b) Does the use of TENS provide a clinically meaningful improvement of function in Medicare beneficiaries with CLBP?

    c) Does the use of TENS impact the utilization of other medical treatments or services used in the medical management of CLBP?"

Exceptions such as these are uncommon. Take, for instance, the CMS coverage decision for acupuncture:

> Indications and Limitations of Coverage
>
> Although acupuncture has been used for thousands of years in China and for decades in parts of Europe, it is a new agent of unknown use and efficacy in the United States. Even in those areas of the world where it has been widely used, its mechanism is not known. Three units of the National Institutes of Health, the National Institute of General Medical Sciences, National Institute of Neurological Diseases and Stroke, and Fogarty International Center have been designed to assess and identify specific opportunities and needs for research attending the use of acupuncture for surgical anesthesia and relief of chronic pain. Until the pending scientific assessment of the technique has been completed and its efficacy has been established, Medicare reimbursement for acupuncture, as an anesthetic or as an analgesic or for other therapeutic purposes, may not be made. Accordingly, acupuncture is not considered reasonable and necessary within the meaning of §1862(a)(1) of the Act.'

Other Insurers

After examining the Medicare site, the innovator should explore the coverage policies for the major commercial insures. UnitedHealth [3], Cigna [4] and Aetna [5] are among the largest insurers and each lists coverage polices on their web pages, which are free, easy to navigate and will give you an excellent view of what is covered as well as why a device, procedure or treatment might not be covered. Aetna's policy bulletins are particularly useful as they provide extensive discussion of how Aetna reached their decision and the citations to the literature upon which they relied.

---

[3] http://goo.gl/0fvaa
[4] http://goo.gl/9ER169
[5] http://goo.gl/objijW

Two other sources can be consulted as they both provided detailed responses to the basic question asked by the insurers. The first are the evaluations performed by the BlueCross BlueShield Technology Evaluation Center. [6] The second is the California Health Benefits Review Program (CHBEP), [7] which also publishes reviews of medical technology effectiveness. While CHBEP examines a limited number of technologies they categorize the strength of the evidence that form their conclusions.

14.3 Codes

Codes are the second leg of our three legged stool. You may have coverage, but now you need a code. Codes are the language spoken by payers. Without a code you have no way to speak to a payer and no way to get paid. Each year, in the US, health care insurers process over *five billion* claims for payment. Standardized coding systems are essential to ensure that these claims are processed in an orderly and consistent manner.

For example, a first check in your reimbursement strategy should be to determine if there is an existing procedure code that covers the proposed new device or service. The codes are used by clinicians when billing for services. For example ICD-9-CM codes are used for inpatient procedures while CPT codes are used for outpatient expenses. A second check is to see if the standard third-party payors (e.g. Medicare or BlueCross) reimburse for that code. A full reimbursement strategy checks for these and other challenges for receiving payment.

The two things you need to know about codes are when to use which codes and how to get a code if one is not already in place.

The list of relevant code sets is:

1. ICD diagnosis codes
2. ICD procedure codes
3. CPT codes
4. HCPCS codes
5. DRG codes

The remainder of this section describes each coding system and who uses it. This is important as different code sets are used depending on where the service or product is provided.

ICD Diagnosis Codes

ICD is industry shorthand for the International Statistical Classification of Diseases and Related Health Problems, or for short the International Classification of Diseases (ICD). In the U.S., ICD-9 is the standard code set and is

---

[6]http://goo.gl/CqsZhI
[7]http://goo.gl/njNDbS

made up of 14,025 codes providing a system for classifying diseases. The individual codes enable nuanced classifications of a wide variety of signs, symptoms, abnormal findings, complaints, social circumstances, and external causes of injury or disease.

The entire International Classification of Diseases is revised periodically and is currently in its tenth revision, which is known has ICD-10. ICD-10 was developed in 1992 and ICD-11 is planned for 2017. As of 2015, payers in the US still use ICD-9 (which dates to 1975). All payers were required to convert to ICD-10 by October 2013 but that deadline, and subsequent guidelines, have been missed. Therefore, when considering coding for a new product, it would be prudent to examine both ICD-9 and ICD-10 codes.

ICD Procedure Codes

The International Classification of Diseases, Clinical Modification, referred to as ICD-9-CM was created by the CDC's National Center for Health Statistics and is used in assigning diagnostic and procedure codes associated with inpatient, outpatient, and physician office utilization in the United States. The ICD-9-CM is based on the ICD-9 but provides for additional morbidity detail and is updated annually. The National Centers for Health Statistics and the Centers for Medicare and Medicaid Services are the U.S. governmental agencies responsible for overseeing all changes and modifications to the ICD-9-CM.

ICD-9-CM codes can be found at the Center for Medicare and Medicaid Services [8]. Also, Wikepedia has a good list of diagnostic codes [9] and procedure codes [10].

CPT Codes

Current Procedural Technology (CPT) codes, are owned and maintained by the American Medical Association. Originally focused on surgical procedures, the Health Care Financing Administration (HCFA, now known as CMS), adopted CPT codes for reporting physician services for Medicare Part B Benefits and for reporting outpatient surgical procedures.

CPT codes are divided into three categories:

Category I Category I codes are assigned to procedures that are deemed to be within the scope of medical practice across the US. In general, such codes report services whose effectiveness is well supported in the medical literature and whose constituent parts have received clearance from the US Food and Drug Administration (FDA).

---

[8]http://goo.gl/n81cvn
[9]http://goo.gl/RC78W
[10]http://goo.gl/XaHl9n

Category II Category II codes are tracking codes designed for the measurement of performance improvement. The concept is that the use of these codes should facilitate the administration of quality improvement projects by allowing for standardized reporting that captures the performance of services designated as subject to process improvement efforts.

Category III Category III codes are temporary codes for new or emerging technology or procedures. Such codes are important for data collection and serve to support the inclusion of new or emergency technology in standard medical practice.

The AMA provides the following guidance for seeking a Category I code.

A proposal for a new or revised Category I code must satisfy all of the following criteria:

- All devices and drugs necessary for performance of the procedure or service have received FDA clearance or approval when such is required for performance of the procedure or service.
- The procedure or service is performed by many physicians or other qualified health care professionals across the United States.
- The procedure or service is performed with frequency consistent with the intended clinical use (i.e., a service for a common condition should have high volume, whereas a service commonly performed for a rare condition may have low volume).
- The procedure or service is consistent with current medical practice.
- The clinical efficacy of the procedure or service is documented in literature that meets the requirements set forth in the CPT code change application.

It is useful to understand how new CPT codes come into existence. The AMA CPT Editorial Panel maintains CPT and consists of eleven physicians nominated by the National Medical Specialty Societies, onene physician nominated by the Blue Cross and Blue Shield Association, one physician nominated by America's Health Insurance Plans, one physician nominated by the American Hospital Association, and one physician nominated by CMS. The CPT Advisory Committee is supported by the CPT Editorial Panel and consists of physicians nominated by national medical societies that are part of the AMA House of Delegates.

Proposals for a new code go through the following steps:

1. A specialty society develops an initial proposal. Typically, the specialty society will be most familiar with trends shaping a specific specialty

and can represent important trends driven by technology and changing practice patterns.

2. AMA Staff reviews the code proposal. This preparatory step confirms that the issue has not been previously addressed and that all of the documentation is in place.

3. The CPT Specialty Advisory Panel then reviews the code proposal. Their comments are then shared with all participants in the process, but not with the general public.

4. The CPT Editorial Panel then reviews the code proposal at its regularly scheduled meeting. The group can approve the code, table the proposal, or reject the proposal.

5. Approved Category 1 codes are then submitted to the Relative Value Scale Update Committee who assigns relative value units (RVUs) for all Category 1 CPT codes.

The last step is important as a new code does not always result in a payment; there are numerous codes assigned a zero payment.

All CPT Category III codes are removed after five years from the time of publication. If the original requesters of the code want to continue use of the code, they must submit a proposal for continuing the code or promoting it to Category I.

HCPCS Codes

The Healthcare Common Procedure Coding System was developed by HCFA (now CMS) to cover a variety of services, supplies, and equipment that are not identified by CPT codes. These are called Level II HCPCS codes. Since 2003, there have been two levels of HCPCS. Level I include the standard CPT codes and Level II include non-physician services such as ambulance services and prosthetic devices, and items and supplies and non-physician services not covered by CPT codes.

DRG Codes

Diagnosis Related Groups (DRGs) are a means of classifying patients likely to need a similar level of hospital resources for their care and are an effort to quantify hospital care. Each patient discharged from a hospital is assigned a single DRG and each DRG code was designed to represent "medically meaningful" groups of patients. Thus, all patients in the same DRG are expected to display a set of clinical responses which will, on average, result in equal use of hospital resources.

Four guiding principles were established when the DRG system was formed:

- The patient characteristics used in the DRG definition should be limited to information routinely collected on the hospital billing form.

- There should be a manageable number of DRGs that encompass all patients seen on an inpatient basis.
- Each DRG should contain patients with a similar pattern of resource intensity.
- Each DRG should contain patients who are similar from a clinical perspective (i.e., each class should be clinically coherent).

Each DRG is assigned a weight that indicates its relative cost as compared with all other DRGs. That weight is then adjusted based on a hospital's geographic location, whether or not it is a teaching hospital, the percentage of low-income patients in the group,and whether a particular case is unusually costly. This weighting is used to calculate the payment rate for that DRG.

Prior to DRGs, payments to hospitals were based on the hospital's reported costs which could be arbitrary and unpredictable. By assigning each patient to a specific DRG, the onus was placed on the hospital to work within a more predictable and structured reimbursement system, allowing for a more accurate determination of the type of resources needed to treat a particular group and to predict more closely the cost of that treatment.

The current DRG system, started in 2007, is called the Medicare Severity DRGs (MS-DRGs). MS-DRGs have a three-tiered structure: 1) major complication/comorbidity (MCC), 2) complication/comorbidity (CC), and 3)no complication/comorbidity (non-CC). MCCs reflect secondary diagnoses of the highest level of severity. CCs reflect secondary diagnoses of the next lower level of severity. Secondary diagnoses which are not MCCs or CCs (the non-CCs) are diagnoses that do not significantly affect severity of illness or resource use. There are 745 MS-DRG, which can be found on the CMS website [11].

Recognizing that over time, changes in technology and technique could affect its payment rate, CMS annually reviews data it has collected regarding the costs of the procedures in each of its DRGs and recalibrates the relative payment rates for the DRGs accordingly.

14.4 Payment

Now that you have coverage and a code, you must determine the likely reimbursement for your device, keeping in mind that the reimbursement amount will depend on the location where a service or product is provided. For Medicare, which is where you will find the best information on reimbursement, many procedures have separate rates for physicians' services based on whether they were provided in a facility or a non-facility settings. What all this means is that, while very tedious, you need to know the places where your product or service will be provided and the appropriate Place of Service codes (POS).

---

[11]http://goo.gl/zKnoV6

A device may be used in an institution. Institutions include, for example, hospitals, nursing facilities, some outpatient rehabilitation clinics, and community health centers, to name a few. Here, the institution will be submitting a UB-04 form to the payer and the pertinent codes will be ICD diagnosis or procedures codes.

If the device is used outside of an institution, for example, in a clinic or at home, a request for reimbursement will be made on a CMS-1500 form using CPT or HCPCS codes. This covers services provided by health care professionals (called professional services, which can also have a technical component attached) and suppliers of durable medical equipment. It can get tricky as professional services are paid at two rates depending on whether the service was performed in a facility or in a non-facility. A full list of place of service codes is on the CMS website. [12]

Non-facility rates are applicable to outpatient rehabilitative therapy procedures and all comprehensive outpatient rehabilitative facility (CORF) services, regardless of whether they are furnished in facility or non-facility settings.

Reimbursement for Professional Services and Durable Medical Equipment

For reimbursement for CPT and HCPCS codes, the first place to search is CMS's Part B National Summary Data File. [13] This file is useful in determining the number of times each code was reimbursed during a given year, the actual payment from Medicare and the amount billed amount, the amount the provider of the service asked to be paid. As a rule the actual payment is always less than then the requested reimbursement. However, the requested reimbursement is of value as it is often closer to actual payment provided by commercial insurers. Along with the data file there is a readme file that explains how to use the data files and the meaning of the modifier codes. Modifier codes are important because they may affect the reimbursement that you can expect.

The Part B National Summary Data File has several major advantages over other sources. First, Medicare is the only health insurance that publishes the amount they will pay and what they have paid for different services. Commercial firms religiously guard this information and though it is possible to purchase their data, it is expensive and often geographically limited. Second, the file contains, for each CPT and HCPCS code, on an annual basis, the number of times the code use used, the maximum amount Medicare will pay (called the ALLOWED AMOUNT) and the amount Medicare actually paid for these services/devices (called the PAID AMOUNT). Third, you can find historical data going back to 2000. Fourth, the file has data on Medicare's covered

---

[12]http://goo.gl/M6Xk4L
[13]http://goo.gl/0d50AV

population, which is huge. Fifth, most commercial payers use Medicare payments rates as a starting point for their own payments.

The file also has two drawbacks. First, the file is limited to Medicare Fee-For-Service Part B Physician/Supplier data and does not include information for services provided in the managed care portion of the program (called Medicare Advantage). Second, the file is typically two years out of date.

The second place to look for reimbursement rates is the CMS Physician Fee Schedule. [14] This site provides both facility and non-facility Medicare reimbursement for all CPT and HCPCS codes. An advantage of this site is that it gives the actual payment rather than just the components of the payment, which typically change every year. Be sure to read the associated documentation as there are several options which are not immediately intuitive, such as national payment amount or local amounts.

Reimbursement for Institutional Services

A common thread in reimbursement of services provided in institutions is the move by payers to prospective payment. In a prospective payment system (PPS), reimbursement is established before services are provided. Various systems are used to assign a payment to a code and then a code to a patient. The most notable is the DRG system.

The move to a prospective system was made in response to the rising cost of health care, driven primarily by acute care hospitals. Implemented in 1983, the hospital prospective payment system assigned every patient to a specific DRG based on the diagnosis and treatment. Each DRG was reimbursed at a single rate. Thus, with some specific exceptions, no matter the extent of services provided to different the patients, the hospital received the same payment for each.

The success of PPS in holding down the increase in payments paid to hospital has spurred CMS to instituted prospective payment systems to other areas, including rehabilitation and psychiatric hospitals, skilled nursing homes and home health as well as to ambulatory surgical centers and hospital outpatient services.

Medicare pays for hospice on a per diem rate for each of four levels of care: Routine Home Care, Continuous Home Care, Inpatient Respite Care, General Inpatient Care. Medicaid and commercial insurers have generally followed the lead of CMS and pay for these same services on a prospective basis. Several years ago it was not uncommon for commercial insures to pay per diem payments (i.e. a fixed amount for each day a patient is in the hospital). However, the entire industry has quickly moved to more and more emphasis on a prospective approach.

The relevant file to read is the CMS Medicare Provider Utilization and Payment Data: Inpatient. [15] This file contains, for over 3,000 hospitals in the US,

---

[14]http://goo.gl/amWtqL
[15]http://goo.gl/d0mq7

the number of discharges, average charges and average payment, for the top 100 DRGs (which account for over 60% of all Medicare hospitalizations).

Another valuable source is the Healthcare Cost and Utilization Project (HCUP), which collects encounter-level information from hospitals regardless of payer (e.g., Medicare, Medicaid, private insurance, uninsured). This includes ICD-diagnoses and procedures codes, discharge status, patient demographics, charges, and cost based on a cost-charge ratio developed by CMP. The HCUP national files [16] contain data on about 7 million hospital stays each year, but based on statistical weighting, represents over 36 million hospitalizations nationally. Separate files are available for pediatric populations and emergency departments and ambulatory surgeries. H-CUPnet is easy to use and can be searched by specific ICD diagnosis and procedure codes as well as DRG. These can be sorted by age, sex, payer (Medicare, Medicaid or commercial) and geography. It can also provide trend data for any of these selections.

14.5 The Future

Health care reimbursement is constantly undergoing change, and the rate of change has increased dramatically since the passage of the Affordable Care Act in 2010. The good news is that CMS's new technology add-on payment is still in force and provides additional payments for inpatient cases with high costs involving eligible new technologies. The additional payment is based on the cost to hospitals for the new technology. However, the Medicare payment is limited to the DRG payment plus 50 percent of the estimated costs of the new technology.

Medicare has changed the approval of reimbursement from local determination to national determination. Since 2003, Medicare allowed payment for the routine costs of care furnished to Medicare beneficiaries in certain categories of Investigational Device Exemption (IDE) studies. However, the coverage was at the local level. Effective January 1, 2015 all technology add-on payment requests will be reviewed and approval at the national level.

You are advised to pay close attention to a number of developments. First is the momentum behind comparative effectiveness. Comparative effectiveness is the direct comparison of health care interventions to determine which work best for which patients and which pose the greatest benefits and harms. Over one billion dollars were set aside from the 2009 stimulus package for comparative effectiveness research in the health care arena.

While this may sound non-threating to a new product, it is just the opposite. The move behind comparative effectiveness is better technology at a lower price. CMS has been vocal about not paying for me-too technologies. At their February 2015 New Technology Town Meeting they reiterated their position that, "Section 412.87(b)(1) of our existing regulations provides that a new

---

[16]http://hcupnet.ahrq.gov/

technology will be an appropriate candidate for an additional payment when it represents an advance in medical technology that substantially improves, relative to technologies previously available, the diagnosis or treatment . . . ". Commercial payers have been echoing the same sentiment.

Second is the move to increase the share of financial risk facing providers. One approach to sharing financial risk is to bundle acute care episodes. A bundled payment is a single payment to providers or health care facilities or both for all services to treat a given condition or treatment as well as costs associated with preventable complications. Another approach is Accountable Care Organizations (ACOs), where groups of providers would assume more, if not all the financial risk of caring for patients. Under these scenarios, providers could receive a single capitated payment for each person on their ACO or, at a minimum, take on a substantial portion of the risk. In January 2015, Modern Health Care reported that, ". . . HHS pledged that half of Medicare spending outside of managed care—roughly $360 billion last year—would be funneled through accountable care and other new payment arrangements by 2018. Separately, mid-March of 2015, a coalition of health systems, insurers and employers including Trinity and Aetna, called the Health Care Transformation Task Force, vowed that 75% of their business would be tied to new financial incentives by 2020."

What this means is that your new technology will need to be both better and less expensive. Premium pricing will be difficult to negotiate and second to market me-too technologies will need to compete on price.

Coverage will remain critically important, but will be based more and more on the ability of the technology to create true value either through better pricing or better performance or, preferably, both. Codes will continue to be the coin of the realm but the transition to ICD-10 will be tenuous and will need to be carefully navigated.

In the past reimbursement was a tedious and time consuming process. In the future, it will require analytic and rhetorical skills to prove that a new technology is worthy of reimbursement.

15 Funding Your Idea

William Durfee, University of Minnesota

Why Investors Matter

- Investors move money from those who have it (the investors) to those with the ideas (you)
- Can take the risk

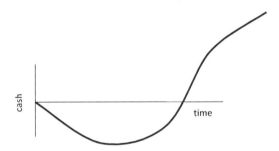

You need investors because a product development activity has negative cash flow for a long period of time, and you don't have the $ to fund developing your idea.

Investors are seeking:

- Disruptive technology
- Chronic disease solutions
- Markets > $1B
- Clear reimbursement path
- Potential for product platform
- Strong management team

Reasons that investors might not like your idea include: market is small, technology is incremental, regulatory approval is uncertain, reimbursement is uncertain, no working prototype, no evidence that it works, no one other than the inventor is excited about the idea.

15.1 Funding Sources

The most important initial funding source is you. Investing in your own project is the best evidence that you believe in what you are doing and are willing to assume some of the risk; a strong signal to early investors. This does not mean mortgage your house because you need to be sensible about the risk. It does mean, if possible, funding the first, low-resolution prototype out of your own pocket.

Often the next stage is people who you know: your family and friends. Again the sums will be small, but could be sufficient to fund a second prototype or to cover the expenses related to filing a patent. The advantage of the FFF funding network is that these investors typically are not interested in owning a part of your venture but rather are motivated by wanting you to succeed and you eventually paying back their no-interest loan. The disadvantage is if you ask too much and are unable to repay, you run the risk of permanently damaging important relationships.

The next step up in funding is turning to private sources, starting with angel investors. Angels are solo or groups that invest in high-risk projects that could have a high rate of return. Angels are investing their own money. To reach this group, you will need a good pitch and a business plan. Angels are generally smart, seasoned investors and will do their due diligence investigation to determine if your product and your plan has merit.

Venture capital funds are the next source and is where significant funds can start to flow. VCs are fund managers who invest other people's money, and are professionals who will take a hard look at your proposition. VC funding often requires that you give up partial control of your company. For example, VC investment can come with the stipulation that the VC fund name a seasoned CEO to run the emerging company.

Non-Traditional Sources

In the U.S., startup and pre-startup companies can receive funding through the federal government SBIR program. For medical devices, NIH, NSF and

DOD do most of the SBIR funding for med tech startups. The advantage of this funding is that it is non-dilutive and comes with no strings attached. The disadvantage is that applying for the funds requires writing a science-based proposal that will be reviewed by academics, having to wait six to nine months before finding out whether the proposal is awarded and having to meet government regulations for entities receiving government money.

Crowdfunding options such as Kickstarter are an increasingly common way to fund early-stage product ideas and could be useful for certain types of products. While Kickstarter does not fund medical devices, emerging sites such as MedStartr do fund devices. Current crowdfunding sites work on a donation principle. It is likely that in the U.S. with new SEC rules that take effect in 2014, crowdfunding can be used to raise capital, although it will come with stringent SEC regulations.

Exit Options

Most inventors are not interested in taking their idea into a fully formed public or private stand-alone and instead are thinking about the appropriate exit strategy, which often means selling or licensing their idea. Of course the dream is to sell a napkin sketch for millions of dollars, but in reality that never happens. The selling price of your idea directly depends on how much work you have done to prove its value through protecting, prototyping and validation. Protecting means you should have at least a provision patent filed; a full patent application filed is even better; an issued patent is best. Prototyping means that you have built one or more physical versions of your concept. Validation means you have bench tested or animal model tested your prototype to determine if it works to its intended purpose. In addition, you should have done some work to determine the market feasibility of the concept (who needs it and why) and have some idea of what the product might cost. The more evidence you have that your product concept has value, the better your position will be when negotiating a license or sale of the idea. The bottom line is that the further you are along the innovation process, the more valuable your concept will be. On the other hand, moving along the process requires time and money from the inventor.

16 Business Plans

William Durfee, University of Minnesota

Business Plan

- Is the roadmap for business success
- Is for internal communication, to guide the company
- Is for external communication, to convince investors
- Defines specific business objectives
- Is focused and clear
- Is continually under revision

The business plan tells a compelling story and explains who, what and why. The plan describes the steps that will be taken to turn the current opportunity into a viable business.

Because the plan describes specific business goals, which include metrics and dates, it is used as an internal planning document to guide the project.

The plan is used to communicate the business vision, strategy and tactics to potential investors. It is the backup document for the idea pitch.

Writing the plan is an exercise in discipline for the fledgling company.

The length of the plan does not determine its quality so keep it short and to the point.

Resources

- Entreprenuer.com, Your Business Plan Guide (http://goo.gl/ohKlj)
- Inc.com, How to Write a Great Business Plan (http://goo.gl/lbFTO)

Typical Business Plan Content

1. Executive Summary
   - Summarize the business opportunity. State what you want. Often, the only page of your plan that is read. Must be compelling
2. Business Description
   - Describe the focus of the business and the market needs the business will satisfy. Describe your product and explain how your product meets the needs. For a medical device, provide an overview of the disease state your product will treat. List the people who will use your product. Explain why your solution is better than the competition. Describe your intellectual property.
3. Market Analysis
   - Describe your industry, including size and historic growth patterns. Narrow to the target market for your product. Explain how purchasing decisions are made.
4. Sales and Marketing
   - Describe how your product will be sold. Describe how customers will be identified and educated so that they will be convinced to purchase.
5. Finances
   - Honest forecast of sales, including market share. State assumptions. Include cost and pricing strategy.
6. Management Team
   - Describe the skill set of the key people on your team, including outside scientific and financial advisors.
7. Medical products
   - Add regulatory strategy, reimbursement strategy and clinical studies.

- U.S. Small Business Adminstration, Create Your Business Plan (`http://goo.gl/GxH9S`)

Books:

- D. Bangs, Business Plans Made Easy (`http://goo.gl/fPqPL`)
- S. Rich, Business Plans That Win $$$ (`http://goo.gl/m0Y1h`)
- T. Berry, The Plan-As-You-Go Business Plan (`http://goo.gl/bE4MQ`)
- D. Gumpert, Burn Your Business Plan (`http://amzn.com/0970118155`)
- A. Osterwalder, Business Model Generation (`http://amzn.com/0470876417`)

17 Pitching Your Idea

Tim Laske, Medtronic

Pitching Your Idea

- Know your audience
- Know what you are asking
- Know your technology
- Know your competitors
- Have 5 second, 30 second and 30 minute versions
- State your goal
- Leave ½ the time for discussion

The basics

"Pitching your idea" means you have an opportunity to present your concept for a new medical device to potential investors, to a company that might acquire your startup enterprise, or to management if you are in an established company. No matter which situation you are in, these rules apply:

1. Know what you want to accomplish with the pitch
2. Understand your potential investor/acquirer
3. Be clear on the value you provide
4. Be clear on what you want
5. Leave adequate time for discussion

Most importantly, know what you want to accomplish. The presentation must support your goals and don't spent too much time on the technology because they will care more about the value it provides than the engineering behind the concept. Is the goal to inform? To update? To convince? To buy? To sell? To impress your boss?

Time Matters

Time matters when pitching because you will never have enough. Sometimes you will have five minutes, some times you will have two hours. No matter how much time you have, don't waste it. If you can present everything in an hour, do so; less is better. Even though you won't have enough time, make sure to leave adequate time for discussion. A rule of thumb is 60-40 for per cent presentation and discussion. So if you have an hour, your presentation should be about 35 minutes.

Understand Your Audience

The "Sweet Spot" for an Opportunity
Is your idea at the intersection in the eyes of your potential partner?

Do your homework on your potential investor/acquirer prior to the meeting, including finding out who they are, what they need and why they might want to listen to the opportunity you plan to present.

Your audience might be a potential partner so determine their competencies and how you might complement them. Find out some of their past failures and their current financial position.

Do not try to pitch the CEO of the target company, instead your entry point to the company are those whose job it is to evaluate business opportunities.

Be Clear on Your Value

Be clear on the value you provide and be explicit about what you are asking for. You should have reasonable estimates, backed up by data from credible

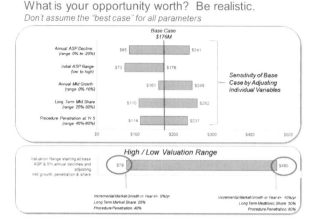

sources, of your clinical or market value, including your competitive advantage. Your investment or acquisition audience will likely know the market space as well, and maybe even better than you, so do your homework.

You should be clear on what risk has been eliminated from your opportunity and what risk remains. In general, you want to burn down the risk early and failing fast is far better than failing later.

And, don't be tempted to oversell your opportunity, which typically takes the form of stating you will capture wildly optimistic market share or that only mop up work remains to get to product launch. Because more technology equals more hurdles, more technology generally means higher inherent risk. For example, new biomaterials used in a Class III device always involves high risk.

Keep in mind that decisions rarely occur in the pitch meeting so stating what you want during the meeting is even more important.

Anticipate Their Questions

Anticipate their questions by finding out what are their top three issues, and then address those three issues in your pitch. For example, project risk will generally be one of their questions.

Your IP position is likely to be another question. State the strength of your IP portfolio, remembering that even granted claims can be proven invalid. Make sure there is absolute clarity on ownership of your IP. Think carefully about whether and how your IP can be designed around. In fact try the exercise of designing around yourself, before others do so.

Cater to Your Audience

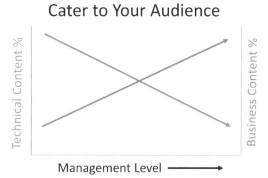

Communicating Complex Ideas

New medical device concepts are complex and your audience may not be experts, so use all the tools available to you to help you tell your story. This includes demonstration hardware, animations, video from using a prototype and explanation of predicate products. If they do not understand the opportunity ... it is Game Over.

Know What You Want

If you say, "We are open to a number of deal structures," your audience will hear, "We don't know what we want." So instead, be clear on what you want: A passive investment? A strategic investment? Do you want to be acquired?

Pitch Tips

- Use your strongest presenter(s), who may not be your company CEO and may not be your chief engineer.

- In your pitch, you are selling the investment, not the product.

- Short forms of the pitch are equally important. Can you make a compelling statement for your idea in one sentence?

- Spend no time describing how hard it was to develop the product.

- Cite credible sources to back up your assertions.

- Format every slide with the title making your point and the body of the slide providing evidence to back up your assertion.

- Use pictures and graphs whenever possible.

- Come prepared and arrive early. (But expect the meeting to start late.)

- Dress appropriately.

- Be humble but confident; prepared but not scripted.

- Practice, practice, practice!

18 Resources

Recommended Resources

Zenios, Makower, Yock, *Biodesign* Excellent text describing the process of innovating medical technologies. Highly recommended.

Ulrich, Eppinger, *Product Design and Development* One of the best texts on product development process. Not specific to medical technology. Highly recommended.

Kelly, *The Art of Innovation* One of the founders of IDEO discusses innovation.

Norman, *The Design of Everyday Things* A classic on usability.

Christensen, *The Innovators Dilemma* A Harvard professor argues that companies must adopt new technology to meet unstated needs.

Cooper, *Winning at New Products* Describes the Stage-Gate and other product development processes.

Kramme, Hoffmann, Pozos, *Handbook of Medical Technology* Seventy four chapters covering a broad range of medical devices.

Iaizzo, *Handbook of Cardiac Anatomy, Physiology and Devices* Comprehensive coverage of cardiac physiology and medical devices.

Kullmann, *The Inventor's Guide for Medical Technology* Short book on medical device innovation process.

Stanford Design School, bootcamp bootleg, `http://goo.gl/xbz6R` Design process methods from the Stanford d.school, a leader in design thinking.

Atlas of Human Cardiac Anatomy, `http://goo.gl/oFXmuW` Comprehensive resource
for cardiac anatomy including video images inside a beating heart.

Also

Iaizzo, Bianco, Hill, St. Louis, *Heart Valves: From Design to Clinical Implementation*
Comprehensive text on the physiology, anatomy, design and performance of
heart valves.

Baura, *Medical Device Technologies* Medical device design from an engineering
view.

Ries, *The Lean Startup:* Overview of the lean startup methodology. A quick read.